Soy-Glazed Salmon
with Ginger (page 90)

WILLIAMS
SONOMA

CALIFORNIA

EVERYDAY
INSTANT POT®

ALEXIS MERSEL

PHOTOGRAPHY BY
ERIN SCOTT

weldonowen

CONTENTS

Cinnamon French Toast
(page 25)

COOKING UNDER PRESSURE

Writing this book turned everything I knew about cooking on its head—in a good way. I went to culinary school in Europe, where I studied classic French cooking techniques along with cuisines from around the world. I don't own a slow cooker (although my mom has tried to give me one on many occasions) but instead use old-school cast-iron Dutch ovens (I own five) to cook almost anything and everything. So when the Instant Pot® came into my life, I will fully admit that I was a bit intimidated—and intrigued.

I love slow-cooked meats. So much so that I'm known in my circle of friends for my pork carnitas and my beef brisket, the latter of which is personally transported to me by a dear friend with Austin, Texas connections. My husband, a good midwesterner, loves anything with the word "pulled" in the recipe name. After tacos, soup is my favorite food group. About once a month, I spend an entire Sunday making homemade stock. I have a silent fear of cooking rice, even though I've made it many times, and I never cook dried beans because, I'll be honest, I always forget to soak them. So there were many reasons why I was excited about this new machine. Dare I say my expectations were met, and often exceeded, when I finally took the Instant Pot® plunge. The meat was perfectly cooked and tender, soups took a fraction of the time, and I'm finally making rice with dinner.

Whether you're a first-time Instant Pot®-er or have been using it for a while and are in search of new dishes, this book is for you. Packed with more than sixty recipes for every meal of the day, it will reveal new ways to tackle classics as well as some unexpected new favorites (cheesecake with a no-bake crust, anyone?). Now I can actually get dinner on the table relatively quickly after a full day of work, and it tastes delicious. (Not to mention the money we save by not ordering as much takeout.) As with any cooking tool, it's important to understand how the pot works before you get started (see the primer on page 8). Never one to cut corners when it comes to food, I've included bonus steps throughout the book where I felt that putting in a little extra time goes a long way, and a variety of helpful tips to make life easier in the kitchen. Because after all, cooking should be fun, and no-fuss, fast, set-and-forget cooking should be just awesome. I hope you enjoy your Instant Pot® adventure as much as I am enjoying mine.

Bon appètit!

INSTANT POT® PRIMER

Welcome to a new world of fast, even, and flavorful cooking. The Instant Pot® combines the power of a pressure cooker, slow cooker, rice cooker, and yogurt maker into one countertop machine. The key to making the most of it is not only learning how to use it but also knowing what cooks best in it.

So what *is* all the fuss about? In a nutshell, the Instant Pot® cuts cooking to a fraction of the time, making traditionally long-simmering dishes at record speed. Meat is always tender and never dried out, because the pressure seals the liquid into the pot—and into the meat. Hearty grains and beans with typically long soaking and cooking times are ready for dinner without a lot of prep or planning. Soups come together in minutes, not hours, making a cozy weekend favorite possible any night of the week.

HOW DOES IT WORK?

The tightly sealed pot boils liquid quickly, then traps the steam and generates pressure. With pressure cooking, heat is very evenly, deeply, and quickly distributed. The machine is available in a selection of models and sizes, each with slightly different cooking features and programs. A general rule of thumb regarding size is if you're primarily cooking for 4 to 6 people, a model with a 6-quart (6-L) capacity should be sufficient, but if you're often feeding larger crowds of 8 or more, an 8-quart (8-L) capacity might be more useful. The recipes in this book were developed and tested using the Duo Plus 6-Quart Instant Pot®. If you've just purchased an Instant Pot®, read the user manual first to get

comfortable with your model's specific parts, buttons, settings, and indicator lights. Here are some key points to know before you start.

FUNCTIONS & SETTINGS

Each model has slightly different cooking features, with up to sixteen different cooking programs to choose from, depending on the model. Since not all models have all settings, most of the recipes in this book use the manual pressure cook setting.

Essentially, you can sauté, sear, steam, simmer, slow-cook, pressure-cook, and braise in this machine. The two most common functions used in these recipes are Pressure Cook and Sauté. You will discover that recipes often use both, with many starting with a sauté step, followed by pressure cooking, and finishing on the sauté function once again. It might seem like a lot of fuss, but once you get the hang of it, it won't feel that way at all. Just think about all the time and effort you are saving by not transferring food from pot to pot or stove to oven and back again!

Most models also have settings specific to a type of food, such as Soup/Broth, Meat/Stew, Bean/Chili, Cake, Egg, Rice, Multigrain, Porridge, and Yogurt. These settings have built-in automatic

programs set to the amount of time and pressure level needed for most ingredients in that category, but you can adjust them as needed. Experiment with these for the recipes you cook often—they might help popular dishes in your household become truly set-and-forget meals.

Some models also have a Sterilize function, which can be used to sterilize bottles and jars easily and efficiently, but it is important to note that the machine is not safe for pressure canning.

Sauté: This function allows you to sear meat, simmer liquids, reduce sauces, and more, similarly to how you would in a sauté pan on the stove. It has three modes: Less is ideal for simmering, thickening, and reducing liquids; Normal is best for pan searing; More can be used for stir-frying or browning meat. The timer on this function is automatically set for thirty minutes, but in the rare case when you might need it on for longer than that, just press the Sauté button again after it has shut off and continue cooking. Never put the locking lid on while using it.

Pressure Cook: There are two levels for pressure cooking—High and Low. Most recipes utilize the High setting, but pay attention to when a recipe indicates using the Low setting (usually for more delicate foods like eggs or fish). Press the Pressure Level key or Adjust key (depending on your model) to adjust pressure levels, and the +/- keys to change the cooking time. (The Lux 6-in-1 V3 model does not have a low-pressure setting.)

Slow Cook: This is a non-pressure cooking program, where the Less, Normal, and High modes correspond to the low, medium, and high settings in some temperature-controlled slow cookers. It works similarly to a traditional slow-cooker appliance, cooking food very, very slowly with more liquid than required for pressure cooking. You can use this function for preparing your favorite slow-cooker recipes.

Steam: Always use the steam rack that came with the pot, or a metal or silicone steam basket, when using this program. The pot comes to pressure on full, continuous heat, and the food can scorch if it's not raised off the bottom of the pot.

Keep Warm/Cancel: These buttons, sometimes combined into one, turn off any cooking program, allowing you to switch to another program or to end cooking. The former also starts up the Keep Warm setting, which will keep the food at a safe temperature for up to ten hours.

Delay Start: This feature allows you to delay the start of cooking, particularly handy if you want to soak beans before cooking them.

UNDER PRESSURE

The pressure release (also called steam release) has two positions: Venting and Sealing. The pot can come up to pressure only when it is closed and the valve is set to Sealing. As a safety precaution, you will not be able to open the lid unless it is set to Venting. There are two main ways to release the pressure when the program ends:

Quick Release: Manually turn the valve to Venting as soon as the cooking program has ended. Take caution when moving the valve—it's best to use a wooden spoon or kitchen tongs instead of bare hands, and to not put your face over or near the valve since the steam will shoot out quite quickly.

Natural Release: The pot will lose pressure on its own as it cools. The time for a natural pressure release varies depending on the volume of food and liquid in the pot (the greater the amount, the longer it will take), and can be as quick as a few minutes or up to thirty. Once the program has finished, the pot defaults to the Keep Warm setting and will remain there for up to ten hours.

You can also perform a combination of the two, letting the pressure release naturally for a few minutes and then turning the valve to Venting to quick-release the rest of the steam.

Two factors contribute to which method you would choose for steam release:

(1) Whether the dish is hearty and would benefit from sitting longer (such as a soup, stew, or braised meat dish) or if the dish involves delicate foods that require only a few minutes of cooking time (such as soft-boiled eggs, fish, or vegetables) and would not benefit from longer cooking or resting times.

(2) How much liquid is in the pot.

Each recipe in this book indicates the optimal method, whether it be quick release, natural, or a combination of the two. But it helps to understand why you are choosing one over another.

The first factor is often pretty straightforward: as many dishes in this book feature hearty ingredients, the majority will use a natural pressure release or a combo.

The second factor is a safety issue. It's important to know that the steam releases quite intensely out of the valve. So with soups or other dishes containing a lot of liquid, there will be more steam releasing and more potential for hot water splattering over your kitchen or people nearby. So although it might be hard to wait a little longer to enjoy your meal after it has finished cooking, don't be hasty with releasing the steam manually. These recipes err on the side of caution when it comes to soups and other liquid-filled dishes.

LIQUID LEVELS

Unlike traditional slow cookers from which liquid evaporates during cooking, a pressure cooker is completely sealed and therefore does not lose any liquid when cooking. This is important because the amount of liquid needed for some recipes might seem quite low—but don't worry, they're correct for a 6-quart (6-L) pot! If you are using an 8-quart (8-L) pot, increase the liquid by 1 cup. The liquid level accounts for all wet ingredients, including stocks, water, wine, canned tomatoes with juice, marinades, and so on. The pot cannot come up to pressure unless it has enough liquid, but be sure not to fill it more than two-thirds full.

PRESSURE COOKING PRACTICALITIES

- To come up to pressure, the pot needs enough steam buildup, which is created from the amount of liquid in the recipe. (Keep in mind that marinades and ingredients like canned tomatoes have liquid in them, too.)

- The valve might feel a bit wobbly when switching between Venting and Sealing.

- A little steam coming out of the valve is normal as the pot comes up to pressure.

- The program timer will not start until the machine has come up to pressure.

- For safety reasons, you cannot remove the lid from the pot when it is cooking under pressure. All of the pressure needs to be released first.

Fans of the Instant Pot® praise its ability to cut cooking time, transform tough cuts of meat to tender perfection, cook recipe staples like rice and beans in large quantities, and self-regulate a slew of safety features. Once you get comfortable with its basic functions and programs, you can retire your slow cooker, pressure cooker, rice cooker, and yogurt maker because this machine tackles all of those tasks—and more!

GET COOKING

Once you're familiar with the basics of your machine, the fun begins. Don't worry about feeling like a novice in the beginning—the more you use it, the more comfortable you'll become, and the more you'll be able to customize recipes and cooking times to your preference.

The Instant Pot® cooks many things very well—and in a fraction of the time it would take using other cooking methods on the stove or in the oven. The recipes in this book offer a robust collection of favorites for every meal of the day—including dessert!

WHAT TO COOK

• Large cuts of meat emerge succulent and tender—especially tougher and less expensive cuts, which will not only save you money at the store but also time getting dinner on the table. (Learn more specifics about cooking and flavoring meat on pages 50–53.)

• Soups and stocks cook much more quickly, yet develop the same flavors as they would when simmered on the stove for hours.

• Rice, beans (which don't require soaking), and hearty grains are completely hands off—just throw everything into the pot and go.

• Steamed desserts are magically simple—no need to fuss with a hot-water bath in the oven or long cooking times.

• Favorite breakfast dishes, such as steel-cut oats and fruit-topped quinoa, are completely set-and-forget—perfect for busy mornings.

• Risotto and polenta can be cooked without stirring at all, a huge help when you're multi-tasking in the kitchen.

Certain delicate foods need very little cooking time, or no pressure cooking at all. Tender vegetables can be cooked quickly on the Sauté mode, either at the beginning or end of cooking. Delicate fish and seafood only need a bit of simmering time in a soup or curry after all of the other ingredients are cooked and the dish flavors are developed. Eggs cook quickly (in some cases in as little as one minute) and often at low pressure. Rest assured that if any of your dishes come out undercooked for your preference, you can simply re-cover the pot, lock the lid, bring the machine back up to pressure, and cook for a few more minutes. Once the food in the pot is warm, it will take less time to come back up to pressure, so any additional cooking will be much quicker.

SAUTÉING, SEARING & SIMMERING

The Instant Pot® Sauté program mimics how you would use a sauté pan or skillet on your stove—and it's one of the most useful features of the machine. Many meat dishes benefit from browning and searing before cooking, so you would begin a recipe in Sauté mode before pressure cooking.

Chicken Adobo Burrito Bowls (page 77)

A few handy tools, such as a pair of kitchen tongs, a fat separator, and a steamer basket, will make cooking in your Instant Pot® a breeze.

Onions, shallots, garlic, celery, carrots, and other vegetables develop flavors when sautéed in some sort of fat (oil, butter, ghee, animal fat, etc.), which will exponentially increase the flavors of your dish in many cases, especially when a spice blend is also tossed in. Another important use for this program is simmering sauces at the end of cooking. When the pot is in a pressure mode, no water will evaporate (unlike slow cooking or stovetop cooking), so reducing sauces for meats, curries, or creamy soups will not happen slowly over time. Instead, you can simmer them for a few minutes on Sauté mode after the pressure cooking step, until the desired thickness is reached. Adding a slurry of equal parts cornstarch and water will help thicken barbecue and stir-fry sauces. (Always add cornstarch and flour at the end of cooking on Sauté mode, never at the beginning, before food has been pressure cooked, because it can settle and clump in the bottom of the inner pot, causing improper heat dispersion and scorching.)

MAKE IT A MEAL

Many of the recipes in this book provide suggested accompaniments that can also be made in the Instant Pot®. The best approach for these is to determine which dish will come together faster and to cook that one second while keeping the first dish warm. For example, Maple-Bourbon Short Ribs (page 62) will cook for 35 minutes at high pressure, but a side dish of Creamy Mashed Potatoes (page 40) takes only 5. So you can cook the potatoes while you let the ribs rest and develop even more flavor.

TOOLS OF THE TRADE

A few key tools are essential to preparing a selection of recipes in this book. They include:

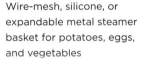

7-inch (18-cm) springform pan for cheesecake and other cakes

1½-quart (1.5-L) round oven-safe baking dish for frittatas, bread pudding, stuffing, and more "baked" dishes

Wire-mesh, silicone, or expandable metal steamer basket for potatoes, eggs, and vegetables

4-ounce (120-ml) ceramic ramekins for steamed desserts

Kitchen tongs for browning meat and transferring it from the pot to a plate; quick-releasing the steam valve safely; and holding a paper towel for removing fat from the pot after sautéing meat

Fat separator to degrease soups and sauces

Standard blender or immersion blender for soups, sauces, and marinades

Steam rack with handles to raise and lower pans and dishes, as well as for cooking eggs (Note: this rack comes included with many models; if yours does not have handles, you can create a sling by folding a long piece of aluminum foil into thirds so it can rest underneath the steam rack and extend up on either side like handles.)

HELPFUL TIPS

Many of the standard rules of cooking apply for pressure cooking, too, but the Instant Pot® also has a few guidelines of its own. It's helpful to read over a few key things to think about before you get started. You'll find bonus steps and tips throughout this book as well, to help guarantee the best results.

- Cut ingredients into the same size so they cook evenly. This applies to everything from meat to vegetables. Size and cooking time are also related, as bigger pieces of meat will take longer to cook. Take note of the sizes listed for ingredients such as chicken, pork, beef, potatoes, and bread cubes, since cooking times are proportionate to the size of the ingredients.

- Cover cake pans, ramekins, and other dishes with aluminum foil when using a pressure setting so that condensation from the steam does not drip from the lid of the pot and water down your dish.

- Pat meat dry before cooking for better and more even browning.

- It's often easier and more time efficient to cook chicken pieces whole and shred or cut them after cooking.

- Freeze beef briefly for easier slicing—this will come in handy for French Dip Sandwiches (page 64).

- Use kitchen tongs to hold paper towels to quickly and easily wipe out the fat from the inner pot during or after sautéing.

- Use kitchen tongs or a wooden spoon to open the steam valve when releasing pressure so that your bare hands don't come in contact with hot steam.

- During steam release, ensure that the pot is at a safe distance from any surfaces that could be damaged by excess water, such as wooden cabinets. Always tilt the lid when removing it from the pot so steam doesn't hit your face.

- The inner pot can get quite hot while on Sauté mode, so sometimes smaller-sized ingredients will cook quickly and might start to stick or burn. If this happens, you can use stock, wine, or water to help deglaze the pot, stirring to loosen the browned bits from the pot bottom (many recipes include specific instructions for this). Use a wooden spoon and stir continually while sautéing to help prevent this from happening.

- Depending on the size of pot you have, the minimum amount of liquid required to create pressure will change. For a 3-quart (3-L) pot, the amount is 1½ cups (350 ml), for a 6-quart (6-L) it is 2 cups (475 ml), and for an 8-quart (8-L) it is 3 cups (700 ml).

- Never fill the pot more than two-thirds full, to allow enough steam to build, or more than half full if cooking rice or beans, to give them room to expand.

- Adding cornstarch or flour before pressure cooking can result in settling and clumping at the bottom of the pot, which in turn can cause improper heat dispersion and scorching. Use cornstarch or flour to thicken sauces after pressure cooking to avoid this situation.

- And finally, one of the most important rules of thumb for cooking is also essential here—taste your food and adjust the seasoning (such as salt, pepper, and other spices) before you serve it. Season meat before browning or cooking it, but also keep in mind that flavors develop throughout the cooking process, especially when simmering at the end of cooking. So use the salt and pepper quantities given here as a guideline, and adjust for your preference.

Pulled Chicken Sandwiches with Kale & Cabbage Slaw (page 81)

Homemade Yogurt (page 26)

BREAKFAST & BASICS

Breakfast Quinoa

This is a healthy, filling, set-and-forget breakfast—put the main ingredients into the pot and let it cook while you get ready for the day. Add more or less milk as you like to the bowls of cooked grain, and vary the toppings according to what's in season, such as berries in the summer and ripe pears in the fall.

MAKES 3 CUPS (585 G) • SERVES 4

Put the quinoa in the Instant Pot®. Add 2 cups (350 ml) of the almond milk, ¼ teaspoon salt, and the cinnamon.

Lock the lid in place and turn the valve to Sealing. Press the Pressure Cook button and set the cook time for 2 minutes at high pressure.

Let the steam release naturally for 12 minutes, then turn the valve to Venting to quick-release any residual steam. Carefully remove the lid and fluff the quinoa with a fork.

To serve, divide the quinoa evenly among four bowls. Pour ¼ cup (60 ml) of the remaining almond milk over each serving, adding more if desired. Top the quinoa with the berries and almonds, drizzle with honey, and serve right away.

1 cup (180 g) quinoa (red, white, or mixed), rinsed

3 cups (600 ml) vanilla almond milk, plus more as needed

Kosher salt

¼ teaspoon ground cinnamon

1 basket (6 oz/180 g) raspberries or 1 generous cup (150 g) mixed blackberries, raspberries, and blueberries

¼ cup (25 g) sliced almonds (toasted, if desired)

Honey, for drizzling

Vanilla almond milk adds a slight sweetness to this typically savory grain, but you can use another milk instead, if you prefer.

Cinnamon French Toast with Mixed Berries

Buttery brioche or challah provide the perfect pillowy texture for a lush breakfast studded with fresh berries (cinnamon-twist challah will take this dish to the next level). You can prepare it the night before, let it set in the fridge overnight, and cook it in the morning for an effortless brunch.

SERVES 6

Grease a 1½-qt (1.5-L) round ceramic baking dish with butter.

In a medium bowl, whisk together the eggs, cream, milk, granulated sugar, cinnamon, vanilla, salt, and lemon zest. Arrange one layer of bread cubes on the bottom of the prepared baking dish so they nestle in snugly. Scatter half the berries on top, followed by a second layer of bread cubes and berries. Pour the egg mixture over the top and press lightly to help it absorb into the bread. Cover with aluminum foil and refrigerate for at least 1 hour or up to overnight.

Pour the water into the Instant Pot® and place the baking dish on the steam rack. Using the handles, lower the baking dish and steam rack into the pot. Lock the lid in place and turn the valve to Sealing. Press the Pressure Cook button and set the cook time for 30 minutes at high pressure.

Let the steam release naturally for 15 minutes, then turn the valve to Venting to quick-release any residual steam. Carefully remove the lid and, using the steam rack handles, lift out the baking dish. Let the French toast cool slightly, then dust with confectioners' sugar, if using. Spoon it onto individual plates and serve warm.

BONUS STEP *After removing it from the pot, sprinkle the French toast with 1 tablespoon of turbinado sugar and bake in a preheated 400°F (200°C) oven for 10 minutes. The crispy top will complement the gooey center, creating the perfect texture contrast in every bite.*

Unsalted butter, for greasing

3 large eggs

½ cup (120 ml) heavy cream

½ cup (120 ml) milk

⅓ cup (70 g) granulated sugar

½ teaspoon ground cinnamon

1½ teaspoons pure vanilla extract

¼ teaspoon kosher salt

½ teaspoon finely grated lemon zest

¾ lb (340 g) brioche or challah bread, cut into 2 inch cubes

1 cup (140 g) mixed berries, such as blueberries, blackberries, and raspberries

2 cups (475 ml) water

Confectioners' sugar, for serving (optional)

Homemade Yogurt

Making yogurt at home allows you to control the quality of the ingredients and the fermentation time, creating a more nutrient-dense result than store-bought varieties. Plus, it's a blank canvas for a suite of delicious toppings. An instant-read thermometer will be useful here, as well as a little patience, since yogurt needs to cook and set for quite a few hours before it's ready to eat.

MAKES 4 CUPS (1 L) • SERVES 6

Pour the milk into the Instant Pot®. Lock the lid in place and turn the valve to Sealing. Press the Yogurt button until the screen says "Boil" and cook until the milk reaches 180°F (82°C), about 25 minutes. Have ready an ice-water bath in the sink. Carefully remove the lid and check the milk temperature with an instant-read thermometer. If it is not 180°F (82°C), press the Cancel button to reset the program, then select Sauté and heat until it reaches 180°F (82°C). Transfer the inner pot to the ice-water bath, then stir the milk until it cools to 110°F (43°C), about 10 minutes. Transfer 1 cup of the milk to a small bowl, whisk in the yogurt until smooth, then return the milk-yogurt mixture to the pot. Whisk until blended.

Return the inner pot to the Instant Pot® housing. Lock the lid in place; the valve can be turned to Sealing or Venting. Press the Cancel button to reset the program, then press the Yogurt button and set the cook time for 10 hours. When the yogurt is ready (the screen will read "Yogt"), carefully remove the lid, use pot holders to lift out the inner pot, cover it with plastic wrap, and refrigerate until the yogurt sets, about 4 hours. Do not stir at this point.

When the yogurt is set, line a large fine-mesh sieve with 4 layers of cheesecloth, place the sieve over a bowl, spoon the yogurt into the sieve, and refrigerate for 2 hours to drain.

To serve, spoon the yogurt into individual bowls and top as desired.

8 cups (2 L) whole milk

2 tablespoons plain yogurt

FOR SERVING
(OPTIONAL)
Honey, toasted sliced almonds, granola, puffed quinoa, sunflower seeds, toasted coconut flakes, chopped dried fruit, and/or fresh fruit

If you prefer firmer yolks, adjust the cooking time to 2 minutes at low pressure, or more for completely set centers.

Baked Eggs with Creamy Spinach & Ham

This easy all-in-one breakfast is the perfect companion to a thick slice of toasted sourdough or country bread. You can skip the ham, or try it with Canadian bacon or crispy pancetta instead.

SERVES 4

Select Sauté on the Instant Pot® and heat 2 tablespoons of the butter. Add the shallot and cook, stirring occasionally, until just softened, about 1 minute. Add the ham and cook, stirring occasionally, for 2 minutes. Add the remaining butter and the spinach and cook until the spinach is wilted, about 5 minutes. Add the cream and ½ teaspoon salt and cook until most of the liquid has been reduced, about 15 minutes. Add ¼ teaspoon pepper and taste, adjusting seasoning as desired.

Press the Cancel button to reset the program. Make four wells in the spinach and carefully crack one egg into each well. Lock the lid in place and turn the valve to Sealing. Press the Pressure Cook button and set the cook time for 1 minute at low pressure.

Turn the valve to Venting to quick-release the steam. When the steam stops, carefully remove the lid. Transfer each egg on a bed of spinach to a plate, top with parsley, if using, and more pepper, and serve with a slice of crusty bread.

4 tablespoons (½ stick/60 g) unsalted butter

1 tablespoon chopped shallot

4 oz (115 g) sliced ham, cut into ½-inch (12-mm) pieces

1 lb (450 g) baby spinach

⅓ cup (75 ml) heavy cream

Kosher salt and freshly ground black pepper

4 large eggs

Chopped fresh flat-leaf parsley, for serving (optional)

Crusty bread, for serving

Potato, Prosciutto & White Cheddar Frittata

Think of this flavor-packed frittata as a super creamy quiche without all the fuss. Naturally gluten-free without a crust, it's a crowd-pleasing brunch or lunch dish paired with fresh greens (and don't forget the mimosas!).

SERVES 6

Grease a 1½-qt (1.5-L) round ceramic baking dish with butter. In a large bowl, whisk together the eggs, milk, ¼ teaspoon salt, and ¼ teaspoon pepper. Set aside.

Select Sauté on the Instant Pot® and heat the 2 tablespoons butter. Add the shallot and cook until just softened, 1 minute. Add the potatoes and ¼ teaspoon salt and cook, stirring occasionally with a wooden spoon and scraping up any browned bits, until the potatoes have started to soften and brown in some spots, about 4 minutes. Add the prosciutto and cook for 1 minute.

Press the Cancel button to reset the program. Transfer the potato mixture to the egg mixture and stir to combine. Fold in the cheese. Pour into the prepared baking dish. Cover with aluminum foil.

Pour the water into the Instant Pot® and place the baking dish on the steam rack. Using the handles, lower the baking dish and steam rack into the pot. Lock the lid in place and turn the valve to Sealing. Press the Pressure Cook button and set the cook time for 17 minutes at high pressure.

Let the steam release naturally for 15 minutes, then turn the valve to Venting to quick-release any residual steam. Carefully remove the lid and, using the steam rack handles, lift out the baking dish. Let the frittata cool slightly before cutting it into wedges and serving. Alternatively, remove the entire frittata from the baking dish by sliding a butter knife along the edges to loosen it. Place a plate on top of the baking dish, invert it, and shake gently to loosen the frittata onto the plate. Using a spatula, flip the frittata right-side-up onto the plate. Cut into wedges and serve.

2 tablespoons unsalted butter, plus more for greasing

8 large eggs

¾ cup (180 ml) whole milk

Kosher salt and freshly ground black pepper

1 large shallot, sliced

1 medium russet potato, peeled and cut into ½-inch (12-mm) cubes

3 oz (90 g) prosciutto, chopped

1 cup (4 oz/115 g) shredded white Cheddar cheese

2 cups (475 ml) water

For a meatless meal, you can skip the prosciutto and adjust the salt to ½ teaspoon during the sauté step.

Hard & Soft-Boiled Eggs

Although cooking eggs in a pressure cooker takes about the same amount of time as it does to cook them on the stove, with this method they will be much easier to peel—and you don't have to watch a pot of boiling water. Adjust the cooking time for how soft or hard you'd like the yolk: 5 to 6 minutes will yield a bright, slightly runny yolk, while 7 to 8 minutes will produce a firm center.

SERVES 1–12

Pour the water into the Instant Pot® and insert the steam rack. Carefully arrange the eggs on the rack, stacking them on top of one another if necessary. Lock the lid in place and turn the valve to Sealing. Press the Pressure Cook button and set the cook time for 5–6 minutes at low pressure for soft-boiled eggs and 7–8 minutes at low pressure for hard boiled.

While the eggs are cooking, prepare an ice bath. When the eggs are ready, let the steam release naturally for 5 minutes, then turn the valve to Venting to quick-release any residual steam. Carefully remove the lid and transfer the eggs to the ice bath. When the eggs are cool enough to handle, lift them from the water. Crack the egg shells and peel the eggs. Use as desired.

2 cups (475 ml) water

Up to 12 large eggs

Strawberry Jam

This delicious, kid-friendly jam is made from only two ingredients and does not require any refined sugar. You can sterilize your jars directly in the Instant Pot® first, and then make the jam in a matter of minutes. If you have extra strawberries on hand, double the recipe—or try other berries when they're in season.

MAKES TWO 8-OZ (240-ML) JARS

To sterilize your jam jars, place the steam rack inside the Instant Pot® and add the water. Place two 8-oz (240-ml) jam jars on top of the steam rack. Lock the lid in place and turn the valve to Sealing. Press the Sterilize button at the normal setting. Turn the valve to Venting to quick-release the steam, remove the lid, and, using tongs or oven mitts, carefully transfer the jam jars to a plate or cutting board. Cover with a dish towel to keep them warm. Discard the water. (If your Instant Pot® does not have a Sterilize button, you can also run jam jars through the hottest setting of your dishwasher, or boil them in a large pot of water.)

Remove the steam rack, select the Sauté button, and add the honey. Cook until the honey is soft enough to stir (cook time will vary depending on whether you use regular or raw honey). Add the strawberries, bring to a boil, and cook, stirring occasionally, for about 3 minutes. Press the Cancel button to reset the program.

Lock the lid in place and turn the valve to Sealing. Press the Pressure Cook button and set the cook time for 3 minutes at high pressure.

Let the steam release naturally and carefully remove the lid. Use a fork to mash the strawberries, or blend until smooth (or still somewhat chunky, if desired) either by transferring the mixture to a blender or using an immersion blender in the pot. If you've used a blender to mash the strawberries, return the jam to the pot. Press the Sauté button and simmer to reduce any excess liquid, stirring occasionally, until the jam is thick enough to coat the back of a spoon, about 5 minutes. Transfer to the sterilized jam jars (using a heatproof jam funnel will help), and let cool completely, uncovered, at room temperature. Once the jam is cooled, cover and store it in the refrigerator for up to 2 weeks.

2 cups (475 ml) water

¾ cup (180 ml) regular honey or raw honey

1 lb (450 g) strawberries, hulled and sliced

Almost everyone is particular about how wet or dry oats should be, so experiment and adjust the amount of water until you find your sweet spot.

Steel-Cut Oats with Three Toppings

Authentic steel-cut oatmeal has never been easier—no soaking or stirring required! Mix and match toppings as you like, or create savory breakfast oats by adding Soft-Boiled Eggs (page 32), sautéed greens, and grated Parmesan cheese on top.

MAKES ABOUT 4 CUPS (1 L) • SERVES 4

Combine the oats, milk, and water in the Instant Pot® and stir to mix well. Lock the lid in place and turn the valve to Sealing. Press the Pressure Cook button and set the cook time for 10 minutes at high pressure.

Let the steam release naturally for about 12 minutes, then turn the valve to Venting to quick-release any residual steam. Carefully remove the lid. Stir to combine the oats with any remaining liquid. To serve, spoon the oatmeal into individual bowls and top as desired.

1 cup (185 g) steel-cut oats

1 cup (240 ml) milk of your choice (dairy, nut, coconut)

2 cups (475 ml) water

FOR BANANA-CINNAMON TOPPING
1 banana, sliced and tossed with 1 tablespoon sugar and 1 teaspoon cinnamon

FOR CHOCOLATE TOPPING
¼ cup (90 g) semisweet chocolate chips or shavings, plus cocoa powder for dusting

FOR APPLE-MAPLE-PECAN TOPPING
1 apple, cut into ¼-inch (6-mm) slices; ½ cup (60 g) chopped pecans; 2 tablespoons maple syrup, for drizzling

Homemade Hummus

Making your own hummus from dried chickpeas that don't even need to be soaked is a thing of beauty—and deliciousness. For a sophisticated presentation, choose vegetables in similar colors and a variety of shapes and textures for your crudité platter. A purple palette, including cauliflower, endive, and radishes, contrasts nicely with the orange hue of the hummus.

MAKES ABOUT 3 CUPS (225 G)

Combine chickpeas, water, and 1 teaspoon salt in the Instant Pot®. Lock the lid in place and turn the valve to Sealing. Press the Beans/Chili button and set the cook time for 40 minutes at high pressure.

Let the steam release naturally, or for at least 15 minutes, before turning the valve to Venting to quick-release any residual steam. Carefully remove the lid and ladle 1 cup (240 ml) of the cooking liquid into a measuring cup. Drain the chickpeas in a colander set in the sink. Transfer the chickpeas to a blender or food processor. Add the garlic, lemon juice, tahini, cumin, 1 teaspoon of the smoked paprika, 1 teaspoon salt, and ½ cup (120 ml) of the reserved cooking liquid. Blend until almost smooth, adding more cooking liquid and scraping down the sides of the blender as needed. With the blender running, add the olive oil through the pour spout in a slow, steady stream until incorporated, about 2 minutes. Taste and add more salt if needed.

Transfer the hummus to a serving bowl, sprinkle with the remaining paprika and red pepper flakes, if using, drizzle with oil, and serve with pita and/or crudités.

1 cup (200 g) dried chickpeas

4 cups (1 L) water

Kosher salt

2 cloves garlic, chopped

Juice of 1 lemon

¼ cup (60 ml) tahini

¼ teaspoon ground cumin

2 teaspoons smoked paprika

¼ cup (60 ml) olive oil, plus more for serving

Red pepper flakes, for serving (optional)

FOR SERVING (OPTIONAL)
Pita bread or pita chips and/or crudités such as cauliflower florets, radishes, endive, daikon, bell peppers, carrots, cucumber, and cherry tomatoes

Quick-Steamed Potatoes

Potatoes are at home alongside braised or roasted meats year-round, but they also provide a quick-and-easy base for an herbed potato salad (see variation below) at a summer picnic or barbecue. This basic method will work with any variety of potato—just cut the potatoes into 2-inch (5-cm) pieces.

SERVES 6

Pour the water into the Instant Pot® and insert the steam rack. Put the potatoes in a steamer basket and set it on the rack. Lock the lid in place and turn the valve to Sealing. Press the Pressure Cook button and set the time for 8 minutes at high pressure.

Turn the valve to Venting to quick-release the steam. When the steam stops, carefully remove the lid. Transfer the potatoes to a serving bowl. Toss with a few pats of butter, if using, season with salt and pepper, and serve, or use as desired.

2 cups (475 ml) water

3 lb (1.5 kg) potatoes, such as russet or Yukon gold, cut into 2-inch (5-cm) cubes

Unsalted butter, for serving (optional)

Kosher salt and freshly ground black pepper

VARIATION

Quick Potato Salad: *In a medium bowl, stir together ⅓ cup (35 g) thinly sliced red onion and 3 tablespoons red wine vinegar. Let stand until the onion softens slightly, about 5 minutes. In a small bowl, whisk together 1 tablespoon red wine vinegar, ¼ cup (60 ml) olive oil, and 2 tablespoons Dijon mustard. Stir into the onion mixture and season with salt and pepper. Set the vinaigrette aside.*

In a large bowl, combine 3 lb (1.5 kg) quick-steamed Yukon gold, fingerling, or new potatoes (see recipe above), 6 thinly sliced radishes, and the vinaigrette and toss to combine. Season with salt and pepper. Top the potato salad with 2 peeled and sliced large hard-boiled eggs (see page 32) and 2 tablespoons coarsely chopped fresh dill. Serve warm or at room temperature, or refrigerate up to overnight and serve chilled.

Eggplant & Olive Dip

Caramelizing eggplant in a little olive oil on Sauté mode before pressure cooking it creates a slightly smoky flavor that pairs well with tangy olives and lemon juice. Serve this Middle Eastern–inspired spread with toasted pita triangles or baguette slices and a sprinkling of pomegranate seeds.

SERVES 4–6

Using a vegetable peeler, peel the eggplant in alternating stripes of skin and no skin, then cut into large chunks.

Select Sauté on the Instant Pot® and heat the oil. Working in batches, add the eggplant and cook, turning the pieces occasionally with tongs, until beginning to smoke slightly and caramelize, about 4 minutes. Transfer to a plate as browned. Add more oil between batches if needed. Return the eggplant to the pot and season generously with salt and pepper.

Pour the water into the Instant Pot® and add the garlic. Lock the lid in place and turn the valve to Sealing. Press the Pressure Cook button and set the time for 3 minutes at high pressure.

Turn the valve to Venting to quick-release the steam. When the steam stops, carefully remove the lid. Remove the garlic cloves and squeeze the garlic flesh into a food processor. Transfer the eggplant to the processor. Add the lemon juice, olives, and parsley and process until smooth, about 2 minutes. Transfer the eggplant dip to a serving bowl and let cool to room temperature.

Drizzle the dip with olive oil and garnish with olives, parsley, and pomegranate seeds, if using. Serve the pita toasts alongside.

2 lb (1 kg) eggplant

5 tablespoons (75 ml) olive oil, plus more as needed

Kosher salt and freshly ground black pepper

2 cups (475 ml) water

4 unpeeled cloves garlic

⅓ cup (75 ml) fresh lemon juice

½ cup (60 g) pitted Kalamata olives, chopped, plus more for garnish

3 tablespoons chopped fresh flat-leaf parsley, plus more for garnish

Pomegranate seeds, for garnish (optional)

4–6 pita bread rounds, toasted and cut into wedges, for serving

TIP *For a chunkier texture, transfer the cooked eggplant and garlic flesh to a large bowl and mash with a large whisk or potato masher, then stir in the remaining ingredients.*

Creamy Mashed Potatoes

The ultimate comfort food is now even easier—and quicker—to prepare. No bulky stockpots of boiling water needed! The potatoes cook in just 5 minutes, and are finished in the same pot with a bit of butter, cream, and a variety of other topping choices using the Sauté mode.

SERVES 6

Combine the potatoes, water, and ½ teaspoon salt in the Instant Pot®. Lock the lid in place and turn the valve to Sealing. Press the Pressure Cook button and set the cook time for 5 minutes at high pressure.

Turn the valve to Venting to quick-release the steam. When the steam stops, carefully remove the lid. Drain the potatoes in a colander and let them stand in the sink for a minute or so to let any excess moisture evaporate. Press the Cancel button on the Instant Pot® to reset the program.

Select Sauté on the Instant Pot®. Add the cream and butter and cook until the cream bubbles at the edges. Pour the potatoes back into the pot. Press the Cancel button to reset the program. With a potato masher or heavy whisk, mash and stir the potatoes until smooth and thick. Season to taste with salt and serve right away.

2½ lb (1.2 kg) large russet potatoes (about 3), peeled and cut into 2-inch (5-cm)chunks

6 cups (1.5 L) water

Kosher salt

½ cup (120 ml) heavy cream

2 tablespoons butter

VARIATIONS

Horseradish Mashed Potatoes:
After mashing the potatoes, stir in 2 tablespoons cream-style horseradish.

Sour Cream Mashed Potatoes:
Melt the butter in the pot, but skip the cream. Return the potatoes to the pot and mash lightly, then add ½ cup (110 g) room-temperature sour cream and continue mashing until the potatoes are smooth.

Buttermilk Mashed Potatoes:
Substitute ½ cup (120 ml) buttermilk for the cream.

Irish-Style Mashed Potatoes:
Thinly slice 3 green onions (both green and white parts) and 1 cup (90 g) green cabbage, and sauté in the pot with the butter until they are softened, before adding the cream.

Cheddar Mashed Potatoes:
After mashing the potatoes, stir in 1 cup grated sharp Cheddar cheese.

Polenta

Creamy and hearty, polenta is often a forgotten side dish. It provides a wonderful base for Vegetable Ragout (page 101) but is also a welcome treat by itself mixed with a bit of butter and cheese. The only whisking required is at the beginning, and then the rest of this method is completely hands off.

MAKES 2½ CUPS (600 ML)

Select Sauté on the Instant Pot®. Add the liquid and 2 teaspoons salt and bring to a boil. Slowly stream in the polenta, whisking constantly so it does not clump.

Press the Cancel button to reset the program. Lock the lid in place and turn the valve to Sealing. Press the Pressure Cook button and set the cook time for 8 minutes at high pressure.

Turn the valve to Venting to quick-release the steam. When the steam stops, carefully remove the lid.

Season the polenta to taste with salt and pepper. Stir in the butter and cheese, if using, and serve.

4 cups (1 L) liquid, such as water, whole milk, and/or chicken stock (page 42 or store-bought)

Kosher salt and freshly ground black pepper

1 cup (160 g) polenta

2 tablespoons unsalted butter (optional)

½ cup (60 g) grated Parmesan cheese (optional)

Homemade Stock

We can probably all agree that any dish made with homemade stock is better than those made with the store-bought version. While meat stocks used to require the better part of an afternoon to prepare, with this method you can shave hours off that time and eliminate the need to keep an eye on the stockpot. Store extra in the freezer to have on hand for quick weeknight meals.

MAKES ABOUT 3 QT (3 L)

CHICKEN STOCK

Season the chicken with the salt. Select Sauté on the Instant Pot® and heat the oil. Working in batches, brown the chicken on both sides, about 3 minutes per side. Transfer to a plate as browned. Add the onion and carrots to the pot and cook, stirring occasionally, until browned, about 2 minutes. Add 1 cup (250 ml) of the water and bring to a simmer, stirring occasionally with a wooden spoon to scrape up any browned bits. Press the Cancel button to reset the program.

Return the chicken to the pot and add the garlic, parsley, thyme, bay leaves, peppercorns, and the remaining 11 cups (2.75 L) water, ensuring that the pot is no more than two-thirds full. Lock the lid in place and turn the valve to Sealing. Press the Pressure Cook button and set the cook time for 60 minutes at high pressure.

Let the steam release naturally. Carefully remove the lid. Pour the stock through a fine-mesh sieve into a large bowl. Discard the solids. If desired, pour the broth into a fat separator to remove the fat (or chill the broth in the refrigerator until the fat solidifies on top, and then remove it with a spoon). Let the stock cool completely, then ladle into airtight storage containers. Refrigerate for up to 4 days or freeze for up to 3 months.

3 lb (1.5 kg) chicken parts (drumsticks, backs, necks, and wings)

2 teaspoons kosher salt

1 tablespoon olive oil

1 yellow onion, quartered

2 carrots, cut into 3-inch pieces

12 cups (3 L) water

2 cloves garlic, smashed

3 fresh flat-leaf parsley sprigs

3 fresh thyme sprigs

2 bay leaves

¼ teaspoon whole black peppercorns

TIP *You can skip the browning step and put all of the raw ingredients into the pot instead, but keep in mind that the flavor will be milder.*

VEGETABLE STOCK

Combine all the ingredients in the Instant Pot®, ensuring when you add the water that the pot is no more than two-thirds full. Lock the lid in place and turn the valve to Sealing. Press the Pressure Cook button and set the cook time for 30 minutes at high pressure.

Let the steam release naturally. Carefully remove the lid. Pour the stock through a fine-mesh sieve into a large bowl. Discard the solids. Let the stock cool completely, then ladle into airtight storage containers. Refrigerate for up to 4 days or freeze for up to 3 months.

2 yellow onions, roughly chopped

2 ribs celery, roughly chopped

2 carrots, roughly chopped

1 cup (90 g) white button or cremini mushrooms, roughly sliced

4 cloves garlic, smashed

4 fresh flat-leaf parsley sprigs

2 bay leaves

1 teaspoon whole black peppercorns

10 cups (2.5 L) water

BEEF STOCK

Combine all the ingredients in the Instant Pot®, ensuring when you add the water that the pot is no more than two-thirds full. Lock the lid in place and turn the valve to Sealing. Press the Pressure Cook button and set the cook time for 2 hours at high pressure.

Let the steam release naturally. Carefully remove the lid. Pour the stock through a fine-mesh sieve into a large bowl. Discard the solids. If desired, pour the broth into a fat separator to removed the fat (or chill the broth in the refrigerator until the fat solidifies on top, and then remove it with a spoon). Let the stock cool completely, then ladle into airtight storage containers. Refrigerate for up to 4 days or freeze for up to 3 months.

3 lb (1.5 kg) beef marrowbones, cracked by a butcher

2 thick slices (about 1 lb/ 450 g) meaty beef shin

2 carrots, roughly chopped

2 ribs celery, roughly chopped

1 large yellow onion, roughly chopped

4 fresh flat-leaf parsley sprigs

1 bay leaf

8–10 whole black peppercorns

8 cups (2 L) water

VARIATION

Bone Broth: *Roast the beef bones for 30–40 minutes in a preheated 450°F (230°C) oven. Add 1–2 tablespoons apple cider vinegar to the pot with the other ingredients and cook at high pressure for 3 hours. Release the steam naturally.*

(The bone broth has cooked long enough if the bones crumble when touched and the tendons, cartilage, and connective tissue have dissolved.) Strain and store the broth as directed above.

Rice

Cooking rice can be a daunting task, not to mention a long one when it comes to brown and wild rice varieties. This method is not only quicker but can easily be adjusted for your texture preference. If you like softer rice, add ¼ cup (60 ml) more water to the pot at the beginning, or let the steam release naturally for a longer period of time.

MAKES ABOUT 4 CUPS (640 G)

WHITE RICE

Combine the rice, water, and salt in the Instant Pot®. Lock the lid in place and turn the valve to Sealing. Press the Pressure Cook button and set the cook time for 4 minutes at high pressure.

Let the steam release naturally for 10 minutes, then turn the valve to Venting to quick-release any residual steam. Carefully remove the lid and fluff the rice with a fork. If the rice feels too moist, place a dish towel over the pot and let the steam evaporate for a few minutes longer, until your desired texture is reached.

2 cups (400 g) long-grain white rice, such as jasmine or basmati

2 cups (475 ml) water

½ teaspoon kosher salt

BROWN RICE

Combine the rice, water, and salt in the Instant Pot®. Lock the lid in place and turn the valve to Sealing. Press the Pressure Cook button and set the cook time for 15 minutes at high pressure.

Let the steam release naturally for 10 minutes, then turn the valve to Venting to quick-release any residual steam. Carefully remove the lid and fluff the rice with a fork. If the rice feels too moist, place a dish towel over the pot and let the steam evaporate for a few minutes longer, until your desired texture is reached.

2 cups (370 g) long-grain brown rice

2½ cups (600 ml) water

½ teaspoon kosher salt

WILD RICE

Combine the rice, water, and salt in the Instant Pot®. Lock the lid in place and turn the valve to Sealing. Press the Pressure Cook button and set the cook time for 30 minutes at high pressure.

Let the steam release naturally for 10 minutes, then turn the valve to Venting to quick-release any residual steam. Carefully remove the lid and fluff the rice with a fork. If the rice feels too moist, place a dish towel over the pot and let the steam evaporate for a few minutes longer, until your desired texture is reached.

1 cup (160 g) wild rice

2 cups (475 ml) water

1 teaspoon kosher salt

Beans, Chickpeas & Lentils

While canned beans are very convenient, they just don't taste the same as the home-cooked kind. Last-minute cooks, rejoice! The absolute best part about cooking beans this way is that they don't need to be soaked ahead of time. For bigger batches, double the quantities of beans, water, and oil.

MAKES ABOUT 3 CUPS (540 G) COOKED BEANS

BASIC BEANS

Combine the beans, water, oil, and salt to taste in the Instant Pot®. Lock the lid in place and turn the valve to Sealing. Press the Beans/Chili button and set the cook time for the cooking time designated in the chart below at high pressure.

Let the steam release naturally, or for at least 15 minutes, before turning the valve to Venting to quick-release any residual steam. When the steam stops, carefully remove the lid. Drain the beans in a colander set in the sink.

TIP *If you would prefer to soak your beans, soak 1 cup of beans in 4 cups (1 L) water for at least 4 hours or up to 12 hours, then cook them in their soaking water. They will cook in about half the time needed for unsoaked beans.*

1 cup (200 g) dried beans, chickpeas, or lentils, rinsed and picked over

4 cups (1 L) water

1 teaspoon canola oil

1–2 teaspoons kosher salt

COOKING TIMES FOR UNSOAKED BEANS

Green, Brown, or Black Lentils	15 minutes
Black Beans	20–25 minutes
Navy Beans	20–25 minutes
Pinto Beans	20–25 minutes
Cannellini Beans	35–40 minutes
Chickpeas	35–40 minutes

MAPLE BAKED BEANS

Select Sauté on the Instant Pot® and cook the bacon until the fat begins to render, 2–3 minutes. Stir in the onion and cook until the bacon and onion are limp, about 3 minutes. Add the beans, water, and a pinch of salt. Drizzle the oil over the liquid; do not stir. Lock the lid in place and turn the valve to Sealing. Press the Beans/Chili button and set the cook time for 25 minutes at high pressure.

In a small bowl, stir together the vinegar, tomato paste, mustard, and cayenne, then stir in the maple syrup. Set aside.

Let the steam release naturally, or for at least 15 minutes, before turning the valve to Venting to quick-release any residual steam. When the steam stops, carefully remove the lid. Press the Cancel button to reset the program.

Press the Sauté button, pour the maple syrup mixture into the pot, and cook, stirring frequently so the beans don't stick, until the beans are tender and the sauce is thickened, 12–15 minutes. Serve right away, or let cool, cover, and refrigerate for up to 4 days (the beans will thicken as they stand). Reheat before serving.

NOTE *Even though using a pressure cooker cuts out the need to cook these beans for hours, they will still have a distinctive smoky-sweet flavor that comes from long cooking. Use real maple syrup for the best flavor.*

3 slices (about 3 oz/90 g) thick-cut bacon, diced

1 yellow onion, chopped

2 cups (400 g) dried navy beans or other small white beans, rinsed and picked over

6 cups (1.5 L) water

Kosher salt

1 tablespoon canola oil

¼ cup (60 ml) cider vinegar

2 tablespoons tomato paste

1 teaspoon dry mustard

⅛ teaspoon cayenne pepper

⅓ cup (75 ml) maple syrup

Braised Chicken
with Fennel, Orange
& Olives (page 84)

MAINS

BUILDING BLOCKS

The recipes in this chapter include many favorite combinations of meat types and flavor profiles—but these are just the beginning. Once you become familiar with your Instant Pot®, you'll be able to create your own dishes by mixing and matching cuts of meat with different flavorings and serving ideas.

When you're just starting out, following the ingredient lists and cooking instructions closely will help you develop your skills in the kitchen. But once you become more comfortable with your machine and an assortment of dishes that work well in it, you're ready to start playing.

Think of the various elements that compose a dish as building blocks for your meal. Just like you might do in some popular mix-and-match lunch-takeout restaurants, you would first choose your protein, then your flavoring or sauce, and then how you'd like to eat it. Perhaps one day it is spicy slow-cooked pork tucked into tacos and the next it is a lemongrass-curry chicken in a rice bowl. The same possibilities await you here.

An easy way to think about it is with this simple formula:

Protein + Flavor Profile + Serving Idea = Finished Dish

You will see many hearty cuts of meat used throughout this book, such as pork shoulder, beef chuck, and chicken thighs. Not only are they economical, but they also lend themselves well to longer cooking times. These tougher cuts are traditionally used in slow-cooking recipes, and also work very well in the Instant Pot®.

Many are interchangeable depending on your preference, or what you have on hand. If you love the Pulled Chicken Sandwiches (page 81), try them with pork shoulder instead. If you become addicted to the Five-Spice Pork Ribs (page 72), use the marinade on chicken thighs next time. Follow the same flavor preparations in the recipe instructions, but adjust the cooking time to the protein you are using (see opposite page for cooking guidelines). Even though not all flavors will work well across all types of protein, for the most part, if it sounds good to you, it probably is!

The next step is deciding how you'd like to eat your new creation. You'll see a plethora of serving ideas for the Chicken Adobo Burrito Bowls (page 77), such as over a salad or in an actual burrito instead of on top of rice. Follow this formula for other dishes and eat them how you like. Quick-cooking rice noodles are ideal for Asian-inspired flavors, and almost any meat will find a happy home inside of a sandwich.

The following pages will help you become more familiar with cooking, flavoring, and serving popular meat types—with plenty of suggestions to get you started. Be creative and mix and match to your heart's content! Not only will you have even more options for dinner, but hopefully you'll also have a little fun while you're at it.

COOKING

The Instant Pot® cooks a variety of meat cuts to succulent perfection in a fraction of the time it would take using traditional methods such as the stovetop or oven. The following is a list of the types featured in this book along with cooking times, so that you can easily swap out one for another as you like.

MEAT CUT		COOKING TIME
	**PORK SHOULDER** Pork is an inexpensive, flavorful, and remarkably versatile meat, and the tough shoulder cut is ideal for braises and stews. After cooking, you'll be able to shred the tender meat with two forks.	*3 pounds (1.5 kg) pork shoulder cut into 4 pieces for 45 minutes at high pressure*
	**BEEF CHUCK** Cuts from the more exercised parts of the steer, such as chuck and brisket, are generally better when cooked more slowly or under pressure, and with moist heat. Chuck is often cubed for stews, while brisket is usually sliced for sandwiches.	*3 pounds (1.5 kg) beef chuck cut into 2-inch cubes for 30 minutes at high pressure*
	FLANKEN-CUT SHORT RIBS Also known as Korean-style short ribs, this part of the beef rib is cut across the bone (unlike the traditional thicker cut, which is parallel to the bone). It is much thinner, and therefore cooks more quickly.	*3 pounds (1.5 kg) flanken-cut short ribs for 6 minutes at high pressure*
	**BEEF SHORT RIBS** Popular in international cuisines, beef short ribs generally need longer cooking times to break down the connective tissue in the meat. This restaurant-worthy cut can also be made at home and is especially impressive when served to guests.	*3 pounds (1.5 kg) beef short ribs for 35 minutes at high pressure*
	**PORK RIBS** Cooking pork ribs under pressure will yield the popular fall-off-the-bone texture everyone strives for. For an extra boost of flavor, coat the ribs in their cooking liquid and broil for a few minutes for a crispy finish.	*3 pounds (1.5 kg) baby back pork ribs for 25 minutes at high pressure*
	CHICKEN THIGHS Available with or without bones and/or skin, chicken thighs are one of the more juicy, and economical, parts of the bird. While the bones and skin add flavor, using boneless thighs eliminates the need to de-bone the pieces after cooking and reduces the amount of fat in the dish.	*3 pounds (1.5 kg) boneless, skinless thighs for 15 minutes at high pressure*

FLAVORING

The real fun begins when you start to mix and match flavors. Make a mental note about which recipes you like the best, both for the types of meat used and the overall taste of the dish. Once you have all the ingredients on hand to make a favorite sauce, it will be quick and easy to replicate it using a different protein.

You will see a lot of ingredients pop up throughout the recipes in this book. Everything from common kitchen staples, like onions, garlic, and ginger, to international ingredients, such as lemongrass, Thai chiles, and Thai lime leaves (also known as kaffir or makrut lime leaves) add wonderful flavors to a dish.

Let the recipes in this book guide you in preparing meals with the flavor combinations that appeal to you. For example, some favorite pairings include ginger, chile & garlic; gochujang & kimchi; tomatoes & basil; and fennel & orange.

Spices can really take a dish to the next level. A little goes a long way with flavor powerhouses such as cumin, coriander, oregano, rosemary, thyme, garlic powder, red pepper flakes, sweet and smoked paprika, Chinese five-spice, turmeric, and garam masala.

Liquids not only help to create pressure in the pot but can also add flavor. Coconut milk,

red or white wine vinegar, rice vinegar, apple cider vinegar, soy sauce, toasted sesame oil, Worcestershire sauce, stocks, wine, heavy cream, and others give each dish a distinct flavor profile.

When you're ready to start experimenting, simply swap one meat for another, following the recipe instructions for preparing the sauce or marinade but adjusting the cooking time to the protein you are using (see page 51). For example, try the glaze from Maple-Bourbon Short Ribs (page 62) on pork ribs, or swap pork shoulder for the beef brisket in BBQ Brisket Sandwiches (page 63). The same holds true for fish and seafood. If you love Thai Green Curry with Chicken (page 87), you could skip the chicken thighs in the beginning and add the same amount of shrimp at the end while the sauce is simmering. Or, for a vegetarian dish, you can replace the shrimp with tofu. There are so many wonderful flavor combinations presented throughout the book that can be used to enhance a variety of ingredients.

SERVING

Last but not least, how will you serve your new creation? We all get a little bored with dishes we cook often—even if they are our favorites. So switch it up and think about new ways to present your kitchen favorites, from tacos and burritos to sandwiches, wraps, and bowls.

Consider the mix-and-match lunch-takeout restaurants that encourage diners to customize meals according to personal taste—there's no reason the same principle can't hold true in your own kitchen. Serve a classic meat dish in a new way, or set out a few options for each member of your family to choose a favorite.

Once the main ingredient has been prepared in the Instant Pot®, serve it how you like. Try it:

- In tacos
- In sandwiches or sliders
- Over salads
- Inside lettuce cups
- In wraps, burritos, or quesadillas
- Over rice or noodles
- Over polenta

For example, the meat from Barbacoa Tacos (page 55) or Sweet & Spicy Mexican Chile Carnitas (page 69) would be wonderful in

a quesadilla topped with Monterey jack cheese and a little bit of sharp white Cheddar. And even though Beef & Broccoli (page 71) is traditionally served over rice, quick-cooking rice noodles would be great for kids—and kids at heart.

The accompaniments for these dishes are often pantry staples, some of which can be cooked quickly and easily in the Instant Pot®, too. Flour or corn tortillas, whole wheat or spinach wraps, brown or white rice, polenta, rice noodles, spaghetti, sandwich buns, and lettuce are all items you likely have on hand and can help influence how you decide to serve a meal.

At the end of the day, it's just a meal, and there will be many, many more to come! So don't get too intimidated or overwhelmed about experimenting with these different preparations. The idea is to create an endless amount of delicious meals that will win over fans at the table—and to have fun while you're doing it.

To quickly char tortillas, place them directly over a low flame on the stove and use kitchen tongs to carefully turn them over.

Barbacoa Tacos

Browning the beef at the beginning of cooking adds a crispy edge to this super-succulent meat, which then gets a sassy kick from the tangy sauce at the end. Inspired by the classic Caribbean-Mexican dish, the meat is then tucked into soft tortillas and topped with fresh lime juice, onion, and cilantro.

SERVES 6–8

Pat the beef cubes dry with a paper towel and season generously with salt and pepper.

Select Sauté on the Instant Pot® and heat the oil. Working in batches, brown the meat on all sides, about 8 minutes total. Transfer to a plate as browned. Add the onion and 2 tablespoons of the stock and cook, stirring occasionally with a wooden spoon and scraping up any browned bits, for 3 minutes. Add the garlic, cumin, and oregano and stir to combine, 1 minute. Press the Cancel button to reset the program.

Add the remaining stock, the chiles and their sauce, lime juice, sugar, cloves, bay leaves, 1 teaspoon salt, and ½ teaspoon pepper, and stir to combine. Return the beef and its juices to the pot, nestling it in snugly. Lock the lid in place and turn the valve to Sealing. Press the Pressure Cook button and set the cook time for 30 minutes at high pressure.

Let the steam release naturally, or for at least 15 minutes, before turning the valve to Venting to quick-release any residual steam. Carefully remove the lid and use tongs to transfer the beef pieces to a plate.

Press the Cancel button to reset the program and then select Sauté. Using tongs, transfer the beef to a large bowl and, using 2 forks, shred the beef. Bring the sauce to a simmer and cook until it thickens, about 10 minutes. Discard the bay leaves. Transfer to a bowl and use a spoon to skim the fat off the top. Transfer to a blender and blend at medium speed until smooth, about 3 minutes. Add the sauce to the beef and stir.

Serve in tortillas or over rice with cilantro and additional chopped onion, if using, with lime wedges alongside.

3 lb (1.5 kg) boneless beef chuck, cut into 2-inch (5-cm) cubes

Kosher salt and freshly ground black pepper

1 tablespoon canola oil

1 yellow onion, chopped, plus more for serving (optional)

1 cup (240 ml) beef stock (page 43 or store-bought)

4 cloves garlic, minced

1 tablespoon ground cumin

1¼ teaspoons chopped fresh oregano

4 chipotle chiles in adobo plus 2 tablespoons sauce

Juice of 1 lime

2 tablespoons firmly packed brown sugar

¼ teaspoon ground cloves

2 bay leaves

FOR SERVING
Warmed corn or flour tortillas, steamed white or brown rice (pages 44–45), chopped fresh cilantro leaves, and lime wedges

Korean-Style Short Ribs

Serve these ribs family-style by setting them on a large platter along with green-leaf lettuce, white rice, and bowls of gochujang (Korean red chile paste), miso, and kimchi. You can cut the meat into pieces, wrap the pieces in a lettuce leaf, and top with a spoonful of rice and desired condiments.

SERVES 6

In a blender or food processor, combine the marinade ingredients. Blend at medium speed until smooth. Place the short ribs in a shallow pan or baking dish and pour the marinade over the top. Cover tightly with plastic wrap and refrigerate for at least 4 hours or up to 24 hours.

Place the short ribs and the marinade in the Instant Pot® and pour the marinade over the top. Lock the lid in place and turn the valve to Sealing. Press the Pressure Cook button and set the cook time for 6 minutes at high pressure.

Let the steam release naturally, or for at least 15 minutes, before turning the valve to Venting to quick-release any residual steam. Carefully remove the lid and use tongs to transfer the ribs to a baking sheet lined with aluminum foil. Press the Cancel button to reset the program.

Preheat the broiler. Press the Sauté button on the Instant Pot® and bring the sauce to a simmer. Cook until it starts to thicken, 8–10 minutes. Spoon the sauce over the ribs and broil until crispy, 3–5 minutes. (Be careful to not let the sauce drip off of the ribs too much, or it will burn under the broiler.)

Serve with steamed rice and lettuce, along with small bowls of miso, gochujang, and kimchi.

NOTE *Flanken cut is a thinner, crosswise cut of meat traditionally used for Korean short ribs. You can use the larger, meatier cut of short ribs for this recipe, too. Prepare the marinade the same way, but set the Instant Pot® to cook for 35 minutes at high pressure instead.*

FOR THE MARINADE
1 onion, chopped

½ cup (120 ml) soy sauce

½ cup (100 g) firmly packed brown sugar

¼ cup (60 ml) toasted sesame oil

2 tablespoons mirin

8 cloves garlic

1-inch (2.5-cm) piece fresh ginger, peeled and sliced

1 Asian or Bosc pear, peeled and sliced into wedges

2 teaspoons freshly ground black pepper

1 tablespoon honey

3 lb (1.5 kg) Korean-style (flanken-cut) beef short ribs (see Note)

FOR SERVING
Steamed white rice (page 44)

Green-leaf lettuce, white miso, gochujang, and kimchi

Meatballs & Tomato Sauce

For a change from the usual pasta, try this served over spaghetti squash—the squash can be cooked while you shape the meatballs and kept warm while you cook them. Or, the meatballs may be omitted for a vegetarian dinner.

SERVES 4–6

To make the meatballs, select Sauté on the Instant Pot® and heat 1 tablespoon (15 ml) of the oil. Add the onion and cook, stirring occasionally, until softened, about 3 minutes. Add the garlic and cook, stirring occasionally, until fragrant, about 1 minute. Transfer to a small bowl and let cool. Using tongs to hold a paper towel, wipe out the pot. Press the Cancel button to reset the program while you shape the meatballs. (This step can also be done in a medium frying pan over medium-high heat on the stovetop, if preferred.)

Line a rimmed baking sheet with parchment paper. In a large bowl, combine the egg, bread crumbs, ½ cup cheese, basil, red pepper flakes, 3 teaspoons salt, 2 teaspoons black pepper, the meat, and the cooked onion mixture. Mix gently with your hands until the ingredients are incorporated. Form the mixture into twelve 2-inch (5-cm) balls and place on the prepared baking sheet.

To make the tomato sauce, in a large bowl, whisk together the stock, tomatoes, tomato paste, basil, oregano, red pepper flakes, ¼ cup (60 ml) oil, mustard, and ½ teaspoon salt, and ½ teaspoon black pepper until well combined. Set aside.

TIP *To form perfectly round and equal-size meatballs, use an ice-cream scoop and then gently roll the mixture between your palms.*

FOR THE MEATBALLS

4 tablespoons (60 ml) olive oil

1 small yellow onion, chopped

3 cloves garlic, minced

1 large egg, lightly beaten

½ cup (50 g) dried bread crumbs

½ cup (60 g) grated Parmesan cheese, plus more for serving

1 tablespoon chopped fresh basil, plus leaves for serving

2 teaspoons red pepper flakes

Kosher salt and freshly ground black pepper

1 lb (450 g) ground pork, turkey, or dark-meat chicken

To make the sauce by itself, put all of the sauce ingredients in the pot and whisk until combined. Lock the lid in place and turn the valve to Sealing. Cook on high pressure for 5 minutes, then turn the valve to Venting to quick-release the steam.

Select Sauté and heat the remaining 3 tablespoons (45 ml) oil. Working in batches, brown the meatballs on all sides, 1–2 minutes per side. Transfer to a plate as browned. Press the Cancel button to reset the program.

Pour the tomato sauce into the pot. Add the meatballs and turn to coat them in the sauce. Lock the lid in place and turn the valve to Sealing. Press the Pressure Cook button and set the cook time for 5 minutes at high pressure.

Turn the valve to Venting to quick-release the steam. Carefully remove the lid and stir. Taste and adjust the seasoning with salt and black pepper.

Serve the meatballs and sauce over spaghetti squash or pasta. Garnish with cheese, basil leaves, and freshly ground black pepper.

FOR THE TOMATO SAUCE

2 cups (475 ml) chicken stock (page 42 or store-bought)

1 can (28 oz/800 g) crushed tomatoes

½ cup (120 ml) tomato paste

1 tablespoon chopped fresh basil

2 teaspoons dried oregano

2 teaspoons red pepper flakes

¼ cup (60 ml) olive oil

1 tablespoon Dijon mustard

Kosher salt and freshly ground black pepper

Spaghetti Squash (page 97) or cooked pasta, for serving

Use a firm, hearty dried pasta shape for this dish, such as penne, rigatoni, or gemelli, which can stand up to pressure.

One-Pot Pasta with Bolognese

Save hours at the stove by pressure cooking the sauce and then simply adding in the pasta at the end. The Instant Pot® comes up to pressure more quickly the second time around, so the second step takes no time at all.

SERVES 4

Select Sauté on the Instant Pot® and add the bacon. Cook until the bacon is crispy and almost all the fat has rendered, about 5 minutes. Add the butter, onion, carrot, and celery and cook until softened, about 5 minutes. Add the garlic and cook until fragrant, about 1 minute. Add the beef, pork, and sage and cook, breaking up the meat with a wooden spoon, for 5 minutes. Add the wine and cook until combined. Add the tomato paste, tomatoes, 3 teaspoons salt, and 3 teaspoons pepper and stir to combine. Press the Cancel button to reset the program.

Lock the lid in place and turn the valve to Sealing. Press the Pressure Cook button and set the cook time for 8 minutes at high pressure. Turn the valve to Venting to quick-release the steam. Carefully remove the lid. Taste the sauce and adjust the seasoning as needed. Press the Cancel button to reset the program.

Add the pasta and water. Lock the lid in place and turn the valve to Sealing. Press the Pressure Cook button and set the cook time for 6 minutes at high pressure. Let the steam release naturally for 15 minutes, then turn the valve to Venting to quick-release any residual steam. Carefully remove the lid and stir in the 1 cup (115 g) cheese. Taste and adjust the seasoning as needed.

Serve in individual bowls topped with cheese and fresh herbs.

5 oz (150 g) bacon, diced

3 tablespoons (40 g) unsalted butter

1 yellow onion, chopped

1 carrot, peeled and finely chopped

1 rib celery, finely chopped

2 cloves garlic, minced

¾ lb (340 g) ground beef

¾ lb (340 g) ground pork

1 tablespoon chopped fresh sage

⅓ cup (75 ml) red wine

1 tablespoon tomato paste

1 can (28 oz/800 g) crushed tomatoes

Kosher salt and freshly ground black pepper

1 lb (450 g) dried pasta (such as penne)

1 cup (240 ml) water

1 cup (115 g) grated Parmesan cheese, plus more for serving

Whole or chopped fresh sage or flat-leaf parsley leaves, for serving

Maple-Bourbon Short Ribs

Smoky and caramelized, these short ribs are definitely comfort food with big flavors. The cooking liquid reduces after the meat cooks to make a rich and addictive sauce that is spooned on top of the ribs. To get a nice brown sear on the ribs, pat them dry before seasoning them, and be sure the oil is hot.

SERVES 4–6

Pat the short ribs dry with a paper towel and season generously with salt and pepper. Select Sauté on the Instant Pot® and heat 1 tablespoon of the oil. Working in batches, brown the short ribs on both sides, 1–2 minutes per side. If the meat begins to stick, add another tablespoon of oil. Transfer to a plate as browned.

Add 1 tablespoon of the oil and the onion to the pot and cook, stirring occasionally, until slightly caramelized, 6–8 minutes. Add the garlic and cook, stirring occasionally, until fragrant, about 1 minute. Add the bourbon and maple syrup and cook until reduced by half, about 3 minutes. Press the Cancel button to reset the program.

Stir in the stock, tomato paste, rosemary, and Worcestershire sauce. Return the short ribs, meat side down, to the pot and nestle them in the sauce. Lock the lid in place and turn the valve to Sealing. Press the Pressure Cook button and set the cook time for 35 minutes at high pressure.

Let the steam release naturally for 15 minutes, then turn the valve to Venting to quick-release any residual steam. Carefully remove the lid and use tongs to transfer the ribs to a plate. Press the Cancel button to reset the program.

Press the Sauté button and bring the sauce to a simmer. Cook until the sauce thickens, about 10 minutes. Taste and season with salt and pepper as desired.

Serve the short ribs over mashed potatoes, and spoon the sauce on top.

3 lb (1.5 kg) beef short ribs

Kosher salt and freshly ground black pepper

2–3 tablespoons olive oil

1 yellow onion, diced

4 cloves garlic, minced

¾ cup (180 ml) bourbon

½ cup (120 ml) maple syrup

1 cup (240 ml) beef stock (page 43 or store-bought)

2 tablespoons tomato paste

1 tablespoon minced fresh rosemary

1 tablespoon Worcestershire sauce

Creamy Mashed Potatoes, for serving (page 40)

BBQ Brisket Sandwiches

Brisket usually takes about three hours to cook, but it comes out of the Instant Pot® tender and full of flavor in one-third of the time. Classic pickles and peperoncini make great toppings on these sandwiches, but you could add some homemade pickled red onions (see page 70), as well.

SERVES 4

Let the brisket stand at room temperature for 30 minutes. Pat dry with a paper towel and season generously with salt and pepper. In a small bowl, whisk together the garlic and Worcestershire sauce. Brush the fat side of the brisket with the mixture.

Select Sauté on the Instant Pot® and heat the oil. Add the brisket, fat side up, and cook until browned, about 3 minutes. Transfer to a plate as browned. Add the wine to the pot and bring to a simmer, stirring occasionally with a wooden spoon to scrape up any browned bits. Add the onion, stock, barbecue sauce, brown sugar, mustard, and thyme and stir to combine. Press the Cancel button to reset the program.

Return the brisket to the pot, fat side up. Lock the lid in place and turn the valve to Sealing. Press the Pressure Cook button and set the cook time for 1 hour at high pressure.

Let the steam release naturally. Carefully remove the lid and transfer the brisket to a cutting board, tent with aluminum foil, and let rest for 5 minutes before thinly slicing against the grain. Press the Cancel button to reset the program.

Press the Sauté button and heat the cooking juices until they begin to simmer. Whisk in the flour and simmer until the gravy has thickened, about 10 minutes. Remove and discard the thyme sprigs.

To assemble each sandwich, add a few slices of brisket to the bottom half of each bun and spoon some gravy over the meat. Top with pickles, if using. Cover with the top of the bun and serve.

1 flat-cut beef brisket (about 2½ lb/1.2 kg)

Kosher salt and freshly ground black pepper

3 cloves garlic, minced

1 tablespoon Worcestershire sauce

1 tablespoon vegetable oil

½ cup (120 ml) red wine

1 yellow onion, thinly sliced

2 cups (475 ml) chicken or beef stock (pages 12–13 or store-bought)

½ cup (120 ml) barbecue sauce

1 tablespoon firmly packed light brown sugar

1 tablespoon Dijon mustard

2 fresh thyme sprigs

2 tablespoons all-purpose flour

4 brioche or soft hamburger buns, toasted

Pickles and/or pickled peperoncini, for serving (optional)

French Dip Sandwiches

This easy one-pot way to cook a crowd-pleasing sandwich is made even simpler by slicing the beef before it is cooked so that everything is ready to go at the end. The cooking liquid becomes a flavorful jus, or thin gravy, for dipping. Onion lovers can add some cooked onion slices on top of the beef.

SERVES 4

Pat the beef slices dry with a paper towel and season generously with salt and pepper. Set aside.

Select Sauté on the Instant Pot® and heat the oil. Add the onion and cook, stirring occasionally, until it starts to soften, about 3 minutes. Add the garlic and cook for 1 minute. Add the Worcestershire sauce, oregano, and garlic powder and stir to combine. Press the Cancel button to reset the program.

Add the stock, bay leaf, beef slices, ½ teaspoon salt, and ¼ teaspoon pepper. Lock the lid in place and turn the valve to Sealing. Press the Pressure Cook button and set the cook time for 30 minutes at high pressure.

Let the steam release naturally for 15 minutes, then turn the valve to Venting to quick-release any residual steam. Carefully remove the lid and use tongs to remove the beef slices from the jus and transfer them to a plate. (They will be very soft.) Pour the jus through a fine-mesh sieve. Taste and adjust the seasoning as needed. Let the jus cool slightly and skim the fat off the top. Transfer to a small bowl or serving pitcher.

To serve, place an equal amount of beef slices onto each roll, pour some jus over the beef, and top with a slice of provolone. Serve the remaining jus in individual bowls for dipping.

2 lb (1 kg) boneless beef chuck, sliced about ¼ inch (6 mm) thick (by a butcher)

Kosher salt and freshly ground black pepper

1 tablespoon olive oil

1 yellow onion, sliced

3 cloves garlic, minced

2 tablespoons Worcestershire sauce

1 teaspoon oregano

1 teaspoon garlic powder

1½ cups (350 ml) beef stock (page 43 or store-bought)

1 bay leaf

4 French rolls, split (and toasted, if desired)

4 slices provolone cheese

Provolone is a classic cheese pairing for this juicy sandwich, but white Cheddar, pepper jack, or Swiss would also be delicious.

Pork & Green Chile Tamales

Allow a bit of time to prepare and cook this classic Mexican comfort-food dish consisting of succulent seasoned meat wrapped in a corn flour dough and steamed in corn husks—it's worth it.

MAKES 12–16 TAMALES

To make the filling, season the pork generously with salt and pepper. Select Sauté on the Instant Pot® and heat the oil. Working in batches, sear the pork until browned on all sides, about 8 minutes total. Transfer to a plate as browned. Add the onion to the pot and cook, stirring occasionally, until softened, about 3 minutes. Stir in the cumin and garlic powder, return the pork to the pot, add the stock and chiles, and stir. Press the Cancel button to reset the program.

Lock the lid in place and turn the valve to Sealing. Press the Pressure Cook button and set the cook time for 1 hour at high pressure.

Let the steam release naturally for about 10 minutes, then turn the valve to Venting to quick-release any residual steam. Carefully remove the lid and, using a slotted spoon, transfer the pork mixture to a bowl. Using 2 forks, shred the pork. Add the cilantro, season with salt and pepper, stir well, and let cool to room temperature. Press the Cancel button to reset the program. Using pot holders, lift out the inner pot, rinse well, and return the inner pot to the Instant Pot® housing.

FOR THE FILLING

¾ lb (340 g) boneless pork shoulder, cut into 4-inch (10-cm) cubes

Kosher salt and freshly ground black pepper

2 tablespoons canola oil

1 yellow onion, diced

1 teaspoon ground cumin

1 teaspoon garlic powder

½ cup (120 ml) chicken stock (page 42 or store-bought)

1 can (4 oz/115 g) diced green chiles, drained

¼ cup (7 g) fresh cilantro leaves, finely chopped

The meat cooks first, then after they are assembled, the tamales steam standing up on the steam rack. This is a great dish to get everyone into the kitchen—enlist friends, family, or kids to help.

In a large bowl, mix together the corn masa mix, salt, and baking powder, then stir in 3 cups (700 ml) of the water until blended. Stir in the vegetable shortening, then knead the masa against the side of the bowl until incorporated. Remove the corn husks from the water and pat dry. Place the husks on a work surface with the narrow ends facing you. Working with one husk at a time, spread about 3 tablespoons of the masa mixture onto the widest part of a husk and top the masa with about 1 tablespoon of the pork mixture. Fold in the sides of the husk to enclose the filling, then fold up the narrow bottom end of the husk over the filling until it is even with the top edge and secure with kitchen twine. Repeat until all the filling is used.

Pour the remaining 1 cup (250 ml) water into the pot and insert the steam rack. Arrange the tamales on the rack, standing them upright. Lock the lid in place and turn the valve to Sealing. Press the Pressure Cook button and set the cook time for 40 minutes at high pressure.

Let the steam release naturally for about 10 minutes, then turn the valve to Venting to quick-release any residual steam. Carefully remove the lid and transfer the tamales to a plate. Let stand for 15–30 minutes to firm up before serving.

FOR THE TAMALES

4 cups (460 g) corn masa mix (masa harina)

2 teaspoons kosher salt

1½ teaspoons baking powder

4 cups (950 ml) water

⅔ cup (140 g) vegetable shortening or lard, melted

16 large corn husks, soaked in water to cover for 1 hour

Sweet & Spicy Mexican Chile Carnitas

This dish is perfect for big gatherings. Set out a large platter of pork along with bowls of toppings, and let guests assemble their own tacos. The sweet and spicy caramelized meat is balanced by a bright salsa verde and a tangy chile crema.

SERVES 6–8

Place all of the chiles in a medium heatproof bowl. Pour the boiling water over them and soak for 30 minutes. (Use a smaller bowl or plate to weight the chiles down.) Drain the chiles, reserving the soaking liquid, and remove the stems and seeds. (They will be soft enough to pull apart with your hands.)

Season the pork generously with salt. Select Sauté on the Instant Pot® and heat the oil. Working in batches, brown the pork pieces on all sides, about 12 minutes total. Transfer to a plate as browned. Press the Cancel button to reset the program. Carefully remove the inner pot to pour off the fat, then return the inner pot to the Instant Pot® housing.

Add 1 cup (240 ml) chile-soaking liquid, the chiles, and the pork, nestling the pieces snugly into the pot. Lock the lid in place and turn the valve to Sealing. Press the Pressure Cook button and set the cook time for 45 minutes at high pressure.

Line a rimmed baking sheet with aluminum foil.

Let the steam release naturally, or for at least 30 minutes, before turning the valve to Venting to quick-release any residual steam. Carefully remove the lid and use tongs to transfer the pork to the prepared baking sheet. Preheat the broiler. Using two forks, shred the pork. Pour the cooking liquid from the inner pot into a bowl or measuring cup through a fine-mesh sieve to strain out the chiles, then pour about half of the strained liquid over the pork. (Reserve the chiles and remaining cooking liquid for the chile crema.) Broil until the edges of the pork are crispy, 7–10 minutes.

Serve the carnitas in warmed tortillas, topped with salsa verde, chile crema, cilantro, pickled onion, and lime wedges alongside.

4 dried ancho chiles

4 dried pasilla chiles

2 cups (475 ml) boiling water

3 lb (1.5 kg) boneless pork shoulder, cut into 4 pieces

Kosher salt

1 tablespoon canola oil

FOR SERVING

Warmed corn or flour tortillas, Salsa Verde (recipe follows), Chile Crema (recipe follows), fresh cilantro leaves, Quick-Pickled Red Onion (recipe follows), and lime wedges

SALSA VERDE

Place all of the ingredients along with 1 teaspoon salt in a blender or food processor, and blend until smooth. Taste and add more salt, if desired. If the salsa is too wet, strain out some of the liquid using a fine-mesh sieve set over a measuring cup (this way you can add some liquid back in if it feels too dry). Store in an airtight container in the refrigerator for up to 3 days.

1 bunch cilantro stems (leaves reserved for garnish)

6 tomatillos, husked, rinsed, and quartered

1 small white onion, roughly chopped

1 jalapeño chile, seeded and roughly chopped

Juice of 1 lime

Kosher salt

CHILE CREMA

Put the reserved chiles and cooking liquid from Sweet & Spicy Mexican Chile Carnitas (page 69) in a blender or food processor, and blend until smooth. Add 3 tablespoons of this chile sauce and ½ teaspoon salt to the sour cream, and stir to combine. Taste and add more sauce and/or salt until the desired flavor is achieved. Store in an airtight container in the refrigerator for up to 3 days.

Reserved chiles and cooking liquid from carnitas (see recipe page 69)

Kosher salt

1 cup (225 g) sour cream

QUICK-PICKLED RED ONION

Put the onions in a medium bowl, add a pinch of salt, and cover with white wine vinegar. The onion will be ready in about 15 minutes. Store in an airtight container in the refrigerator for up to 2 weeks.

1 red onion, thinly sliced

Kosher salt

White wine vinegar

Beef & Broccoli

So much better than takeout, the meat in this classic dish will practically fall apart on your fork while the broccoli stays tender and crisp. Adjust the sauté time at the end to thicken the sauce to your preference.

SERVES 4–6

In a small bowl or glass measuring cup, whisk together the soy sauce, vinegar, stock, oyster sauce, and sesame oil. Set aside.

Select Sauté on the Instant Pot® and heat 1 tablespoon of the canola oil. Add the broccoli and toss with the oil. Add the water and cook, stirring occasionally, just until the broccoli is bright green and slightly tender, about 3 minutes. Use tongs or a large serving spoon to transfer the broccoli to a plate.

Season the beef on both sides with pepper. Heat 1 tablespoon canola oil and add the beef. Brown the beef evenly on both sides, about 4 minutes per side. Add an additional tablespoon of canola oil if the pot gets too dry. Once the beef is browned, transfer it to a plate. Add the garlic and ginger and cook until fragrant, about 1 minute. Add the stock mixture and bring to a simmer, stirring occasionally with a wooden spoon to scrape up any browned bits. Press the Cancel button.

Slice the beef into thin strips (¼ inch/6 mm thick) and return it to the pot. Stir to submerge the beef slices in the liquid. Lock the lid in place and turn the valve to Sealing. Press the Pressure Cook button and set the cook time for 12 minutes at high pressure.

Let the steam release naturally for about 12 minutes, then turn the valve to Venting to quick-release any residual steam. Add the cornstarch mixture and the brown sugar to the pot and stir to combine. Press the Cancel button to reset the program. Select Sauté and simmer the sauce until thickened, 5–7 minutes. Return the broccoli to the pot and stir until warmed through, about 2 minutes.

Serve over rice and sprinkle with sesame seeds, if using.

¼ cup (60 ml) soy sauce

1 tablespoon plus 1 teaspoon rice vinegar

¾ cup (180 ml) chicken stock (page 42 or store-bought)

3 tablespoons oyster sauce

½ teaspoon toasted sesame oil

2–3 tablespoons canola oil

1 head broccoli, cut into florets, rough stems discarded

2 tablespoons water

2 lb (1 kg) boneless beef chuck roast

Freshly ground black pepper

4 cloves garlic, minced

2 tablespoons peeled and minced fresh ginger

2 tablespoons cornstarch mixed with 2 tablespoons cold water

1 tablespoon firmly packed brown sugar

Steamed white or brown rice (pages 44–45), for serving

Toasted sesame seeds, for serving (optional)

Five-Spice Pork Ribs

Barbecuing ribs is often an all-day affair, but it doesn't have to be! This method cuts cooking to a fraction of the time, but combined with the quick broiling step at the end, yields the same results—falling-off-the-bone meat with a finger-licking coating flavored with an aromatic blend of spices.

SERVES 6

Cut rib racks into slabs of about 3 ribs each. Place in a large bowl, season lightly with salt, and set aside.

In a small bowl or measuring cup, whisk together the orange juice, soy sauce, fish sauce, five-spice powder, sambal oelek, and sugar. Set aside.

Select Sauté on the Instant Pot® and heat the oil. Cook the shallots, stirring occasionally, until soft and slightly browned, about 4 minutes. Add the garlic and ginger and cook until fragrant, about 1 minute. Add the juice mixture and bring to a simmer. Press the Cancel button to reset the program.

Pour the five-spice sauce over the ribs and let sit for 5 minutes. Stack the ribs upright in the pot and pour the sauce over the ribs. Lock the lid in place and turn the valve to Sealing. Press the Pressure Cook button and set the cook time for 25 minutes at high pressure.

Line a rimmed baking sheet with aluminum foil.

Let the steam release naturally. Carefully remove the lid and use tongs to transfer the ribs to the prepared baking sheet. Preheat the broiler.

Select Sauté on the Instant Pot® and simmer the sauce until thickened, 10–12 minutes. Brush the top side of the ribs with the sauce, place in the broiler, and broil for 3 minutes. Carefully remove the baking sheet from the broiler. Using tongs, turn the ribs over and brush them with the remaining sauce. Return the ribs to the broiler and broil for 3 minutes.

Transfer to a platter and serve.

3 lb (1.5 kg) baby back pork ribs

Kosher salt

½ cup (120 ml) freshly squeezed orange juice (from 1 large orange)

2 tablespoons soy sauce

2 tablespoons fish sauce

1 tablespoon Chinese five-spice powder

2 teaspoons sambal oelek (Indonesian red chile paste) or Sriracha

1 teaspoon sugar

1 tablespoon canola oil

2 shallots, diced

3 cloves garlic, minced

2-inch (5-cm) piece fresh ginger, peeled and minced

Beer-Braised Sausage & Pepper Sandwiches

An adult spin on a ballpark staple, these hearty sandwiches are updated with sautéed leeks in place of onions, which are then cooked in beer for a richer flavor. You can replace the ale with the same amount of apple cider, if you like.

SERVES 6

Select Sauté on the Instant Pot® and heat the oil. Cook the sausages until evenly browned on both sides, about 6 minutes. Use tongs to transfer the sausages to a plate. Using tongs to hold a paper towel, wipe out all but 1–2 tablespoons of fat from the pot. Add the leeks and cook, stirring occasionally, until they just begin to soften, about 3 minutes. Add 1 tablespoon of the ale to the pot and stir with a wooden spoon to scrape up any browned bits. Press the Cancel button to reset the program.

Add the remaining ale, the vinegar, bay leaves, ½ teaspoon salt, and ½ teaspoon pepper and stir to combine. Return the sausage to the pot and layer the red pepper slices on top. Lock the lid in place and turn the valve to Sealing. Press the Pressure Cook button and set the cook time for 15 minutes at high pressure.

Let the steam release naturally for 10 minutes, then turn the valve to Venting to quick-release any residual steam. Carefully remove the lid, discard the bay leaves, and use tongs to transfer one sausage to the bottom half of each roll. Top with leeks and slices of peppers and the top half of the roll. Serve warm.

1 tablespoon olive oil

6 Italian sweet or hot pork sausages (about 1½ lb/ 680 g), pricked with a fork

2 large leeks, white and pale green tops, halved lengthwise and sliced crosswise

1 cup (240 ml) brown ale or lager

1 teaspoon red wine vinegar

3 bay leaves

Kosher salt and freshly ground black pepper

2 red bell peppers, seeded and sliced

6 Italian rolls, split and toasted, for serving

Chicken & Smoked Sausage Jambalaya

This staple of the Louisiana Creole table makes an ideal one-pot meal. The Cajun "holy trinity" of onions, celery, and bell peppers is seasoned, sautéed, and added to a mix of chicken, smoked sausage, tomatoes, and rice.

SERVES 4–6

Cut the chicken into 1-inch (2.5-cm) cubes and season it with salt and pepper. Cut the sausage on the diagonal into ¼-inch (6-mm) slices; set aside. Seed and coarsely chop the bell peppers, coarsely chop the onion, and cut the celery on the diagonal into ½-inch (12-mm) slices; set aside.

Select Sauté on the Instant Pot® and heat 3 tablespoons (45 ml) of the oil. Working in batches, brown the chicken on both sides, about 1 minute per side. Transfer to a plate as browned. Add the sausage to the pot and cook, stirring frequently, for 1 minute. Add the bell peppers, onion, celery, and garlic and drizzle with the remaining 3 tablespoons (45 ml) oil. Add the Old Bay seasoning, garlic powder, thyme, and smoked paprika and stir to combine. Cook, stirring occasionally, until the vegetables soften slightly, about 3 minutes. Add the rice, tomato paste, tomatoes, stock, and reserved chicken and bring to a boil. Press the Cancel button to reset the program.

Lock the lid in place and turn the valve to Sealing. Press the Pressure Cook button and set the cook time for 8 minutes at high pressure.

Let the steam release naturally. Carefully remove the lid, and press the Cancel button to reset the program. Select Sauté and cook, stirring frequently, until slightly thickened, about 5 minutes.

Ladle the jambalaya into bowls, sprinkle with cilantro, and serve.

1 lb (450 g) boneless, skinless chicken thighs

Kosher salt and freshly ground black pepper

¾ lb (340 g) fully cooked smoked sausage

1 *each* large red and green bell pepper

1 large yellow onion

2 ribs celery

6 tablespoons (90 ml) vegetable oil

3 cloves garlic, minced

2½ teaspoons Old Bay seasoning

1 teaspoon garlic powder

½ teaspoon dried thyme

½ teaspoon smoked paprika

1½ cups (300 g) long-grain white rice

2 tablespoons tomato paste

1 can (28 oz/800 g) crushed tomatoes

1½ cups (350 ml) chicken stock (page 42 or store-bought)

Chopped fresh cilantro leaves, for serving

Chicken Adobo Burrito Bowls

This flavorful Filipino-style chicken is very versatile. You can also wrap the chicken, rice, and toppings in a flour tortilla to make a classic burrito, or serve them over crispy romaine or little gem lettuce for a meal-worthy salad.

SERVES 6

In a small bowl or measuring cup, whisk together the vinegar, soy sauce, and sugar. Set aside.

Spread half of the sliced onion in an even layer in the bottom of the Instant Pot®. Top with the ginger and garlic, distributing them evenly. Arrange the chicken pieces in a single layer over the onions. Sprinkle with ¼ teaspoon salt and 1 teaspoon pepper, then cover the chicken evenly with the remaining onion slices. Pour the vinegar mixture over the chicken. Lock the lid in place and turn the valve to Sealing. Press the Pressure Cook button and set the cook time for 15 minutes at high pressure.

Let the steam release naturally, or for at least 15 minutes, before turning the valve to Venting to quick-release any residual steam. Carefully remove the lid and use tongs to transfer the chicken to a plate. Using two forks, shred the chicken.

Serve the chicken over individual bowls of rice with your choice of accompaniments. Drizzle some of the cooking liquid on top of the shredded chicken, if desired.

½ cup (120 ml) white wine vinegar

¼ cup (60 ml) soy sauce

1 tablespoon sugar

2 yellow onions, thinly sliced

1-inch (2.5-cm) piece fresh ginger, peeled and sliced

6 cloves garlic, crushed

2 lb (1 kg) boneless, skinless chicken thighs

Kosher salt and freshly ground black pepper

FOR SERVING
Steamed white or brown rice (pages 44–45)

Cooked black beans (page 46), diced avocado, salsa, fresh-cut corn kernels, and/or cherry tomato halves

Coconut Curry Noodles with Chicken

Burmese cuisine shares some key ingredients with neighboring Thailand but is also heavily influenced by Indian and Chinese food. Although red in color like the popular Thai red curry, this Burmese-style dish is served over noodles and has its own distinctive flavor.

SERVES 6

In a blender, combine the chopped ½ onion, garlic, ginger, and stock and purée until well combined. Set aside.

Season the chicken on both sides with salt. Set aside.

Select Sauté on the Instant Pot® and heat the oil. Add the sliced onion and cook, stirring occasionally, until well browned, about 7 minutes. Add the turmeric, paprika, cayenne, and ½ teaspoon salt and stir to combine. Add the onion purée and stir to combine. Press the Cancel button to reset the program.

Add the chicken and toss with the sauce to coat. Lock the lid in place and turn the valve to Sealing. Press the Pressure Cook button and set the cook time for 10 minutes at high pressure.

1 yellow onion, sliced, plus ½ yellow onion, chopped

2 cloves garlic, chopped

2 tablespoons peeled and chopped fresh ginger

½ cup (120 ml) chicken stock (page 42 or store-bought)

2½ lb (1.2 kg) boneless, skinless chicken thighs

Kosher salt

1 tablespoon canola oil

1 teaspoon ground turmeric

1 tablespoon sweet paprika

¼ teaspoon cayenne pepper

Look for fresh Chinese wheat noodles in the refrigerated section of the grocery store or at an Asian market. If you can't find them, fresh or dried spaghetti is a good substitute. Serve the curry with a big slice of Meyer Lemon–Gingersnap Cheesecake (page 123) for dessert.

Prepare the noodles according to the package instructions and set aside.

Let the steam release naturally for 15 minutes, then turn the valve to Venting to quick-release any residual steam. Remove the lid and, using a slotted spoon, transfer the chicken to a plate. When it's cool enough to handle, shred into bite-size pieces. Press the Cancel button to reset the program.

Press the Sauté button and add the coconut milk and lime juice and bring to a simmer. Cook until the coconut milk is reduced to your desired thickness, 8–12 minutes. Taste and add more salt, if needed. Return the shredded chicken pieces to the pot and stir to combine.

Put the noodles in a large bowl, add the chicken and curry sauce, and stir together to mix well. Sprinkle with lime zest and serve right away with lime wedges alongside.

¾ lb (340 g) fresh Chinese wheat noodles or spaghetti, for serving

1 can (13.5 oz/400 ml) coconut milk, well shaken

2 limes, 1 zested and juiced, 1 cut into 6 wedges

A slurry is a mix of cornstarch and water that helps thicken a sauce when added to the pot at the end of cooking.

Pulled Chicken Sandwiches with Kale & Cabbage Slaw

What could be better than a backyard barbecue where you don't need to fuss with the grill? The layered flavors of this homemade barbecue sauce enliven tender, juicy chicken that cooks in just 15 minutes. Top with a crunchy kale-and-cabbage slaw and a buttery bun, and you've got the ideal party sandwich. You could swap the brioche buns for pretzel buns, or use a mini version of either to create sliders.

SERVES 6–8

To make the sauce, in a small bowl, whisk together the brown sugar, cider vinegar, tomato paste, mustard, Worcestershire sauce, smoked paprika, garlic powder, cayenne, and dry mustard. Season with salt and black pepper, then whisk in the stock. Set the sauce aside.

Season the chicken with salt and black pepper. Select Sauté on the Instant Pot® and heat the oil. Working in batches, brown the chicken on both sides, 2–3 minutes per side. Transfer to a plate as browned. Press the Cancel button to reset the program.

Pour the sauce into the pot and add the chicken. Stir to coat. Lock the lid in place and turn the valve to Sealing. Press the Pressure Cook button and set the cook time for 15 minutes at high pressure.

Meanwhile, to make the slaw, in a large bowl, combine the cabbages, kale, and red onion. In a small bowl, whisk together the mayonnaise, mustard, and white wine vinegar and pour over the slaw. Sprinkle with the poppy seeds, season with salt and pepper, and toss to combine. Set aside.

FOR THE SAUCE

½ cup (100 g) firmly packed light brown sugar

2 tablespoons cider vinegar

2 tablespoons tomato paste

1 tablespoon Dijon mustard

1 tablespoon Worcestershire sauce

1 teaspoon smoked paprika

1 teaspoon garlic powder

¼ teaspoon cayenne pepper

¼ teaspoon dry mustard

Kosher salt and freshly ground black pepper

⅓ cup (75 ml) chicken stock (page 42 or store-bought)

3 lb (1.5 kg) boneless, skinless chicken thighs

2 tablespoons canola oil

continued on page 82

continued from page 81

Let the steam release naturally, or for at least 15 minutes, before turning the valve to Venting to quick-release any residual steam. Carefully remove the lid and use tongs to transfer the chicken to a plate. Using two forks, shred the chicken. Press the Cancel button to reset the program.

Whisk the cornstarch slurry to recombine, and add it to the sauce in the pot. Press the Sauté button, and whisk occasionally until the sauce begins to simmer. Cook until thickened, about 3 minutes. Return the chicken to the pot and toss to coat.

Serve the chicken on the buns topped with the slaw.

TIP *Skip the bun and transform this sandwich into a bowl by serving the pulled chicken and slaw over steamed white or brown rice (pages 44–45).*

FOR THE KALE & CABBAGE SLAW

1 cup (90 g) *each* **thinly sliced napa and red cabbage**

1 cup (90 g) thinly sliced kale leaves

¼ cup (45 g) minced red onion

¼ cup (60 ml) mayonnaise

2 teaspoons Dijon mustard

2 teaspoons white wine vinegar

1 tablespoon poppy seeds

Kosher salt and freshly ground black pepper

1 tablespoon cornstarch mixed with 1 tablespoon cold water

6–8 brioche or pretzel buns, split and toasted

Chicken Tikka Masala

A mix of Indian spices, chicken, cauliflower, tomatoes, and cream creates a comforting and quick weeknight meal that comes together in minutes. Traditionally served over rice, it could also be used as a filling for a wrap or burrito, or served with a side of naan.

SERVES 4

Select Sauté on the Instant Pot® and melt the ghee. Add the onion and cook, stirring occasionally, until softened, about 3 minutes. Add the garlic, ginger, chile, cinnamon stick, garam masala, smoked paprika, coriander, turmeric, 1 teaspoon salt, and ¼ teaspoon pepper and cook, stirring, until fragrant, about 1 minute more. Add the chicken and cook, stirring occasionally, until cooked through, about 5 minutes. Stir in the tomatoes and cauliflower. Press the Cancel button to reset the program.

Lock the lid in place and turn the valve to Sealing. Press the Pressure Cook button and set the cook time for 10 minutes at high pressure.

Turn the valve to Venting to quick-release the steam. Carefully remove the lid, stir in the cream, and season with salt and pepper.

Spoon rice onto individual plates, top with the chicken, and serve.

2 tablespoons ghee or vegetable oil

1 yellow onion, diced

4 cloves garlic, minced

1-inch (2.5-cm) piece fresh ginger, peeled and grated

½ jalapeño chile, seeded and minced

1 cinnamon stick

1 teaspoon garam masala

1 teaspoon smoked paprika

1 teaspoon ground coriander

1 teaspoon ground turmeric

Kosher salt and freshly ground black pepper

2 lb (1 kg) boneless, skinless chicken thighs, cut into 2-inch (5-cm) cubes

1 can (14.5 oz/410 g) diced tomatoes with juice

2 cups (120 g) cauliflower florets

½ cup (120 ml) heavy cream or coconut milk

Steamed white or brown rice (pages 44–45), for serving

Braised Chicken with Fennel, Orange & Olives

The flavor-packed combo of sharp fennel, hearty mustard, pungent olives, and refreshing orange juice wakes up everyday chicken thighs—a less expensive cut of chicken that becomes mouthwateringly tender in just 13 minutes—making this dish ideal for a big family dinner.

SERVES 6–8

Zest and juice the orange, then strain the juice through a fine-mesh sieve into a small bowl; you should have about ½ cup (120 ml). Add the zest, stock, mustard, and 1 teaspoon salt and whisk to combine.

Season the chicken with 2 teaspoons salt and ½ teaspoon pepper. Select Sauté on the Instant Pot® and heat the oil. Working in batches, cook the chicken skin-side-down until nicely browned, about 5 minutes. Transfer to a plate as browned. Press the Cancel button to reset the program.

Return the chicken to the pot. Add the fennel, olives, and orange juice mixture and stir to combine. Lock the lid in place and turn the valve to Sealing. Press the Pressure Cook button and set the cook time for 15 minutes at high pressure.

Let the steam release naturally, or for at least 15 minutes, before turning the valve to Venting to quick-release any residual steam. Carefully remove the lid and use tongs to transfer the chicken to a plate. Press the Cancel button to reset the program.

Press the Sauté button and simmer the cooking liquid until it starts to thicken slightly, 5–8 minutes. (The sauce will continue to thicken as it cools.) Return the chicken to the pot and stir to coat.

Serve over mashed potatoes, with sauce drizzled on top. Garnish with fennel fronds, if you like.

1 large orange

½ cup (120 ml) chicken stock (page 42 or store-bought)

2 tablespoons whole-grain mustard

Kosher salt and freshly ground black pepper

3 lb (1.5 kg) bone-in, skin-on chicken thighs

2 tablespoons olive oil

1 large fennel bulb, trimmed and cut into wedges (reserve any fronds for optional garnish)

½ cup (60 g) pitted Castelvetrano or Kalamata olives

Creamy Mashed Potatoes (page 40), for serving

If you like spice, add in some or all of the Thai chile seeds when you sauté the garlic, chiles, ginger, and lemongrass.

Thai Green Curry with Chicken

Only a handful of Asian ingredients are needed to create the authentic flavor of this dish. Take the time to find Thai green chiles, Thai lime leaves, Thai basil, and lemongrass stalks at an Asian market or specialty produce store.

SERVES 6

Bruise the lemongrass stalk with the flat side of a knife, then thinly slice it (you should have about 1½ tablespoons). Trim the green beans and cut them in half. Cut the bell pepper into slices 1 inch (2.5 cm) thick. Finely chop the chiles (remove the seeds for less heat, if desired). Mince the shallots, garlic, and ginger; set all aside.

Season the chicken generously with salt. Select Sauté on the Instant Pot® and heat the oil. Cook the shallots until they begin to soften, about 2 minutes. Add the garlic, ginger, chiles, and lemongrass and cook until fragrant, about 1 minute. Add the curry paste and stir until combined. Press the Cancel button to reset the program.

Add the stock, fish sauce, chicken, and lime leaves to the pot and stir. Lock the lid in place and turn the valve to Sealing. Press the Pressure Cook button and set the cook time for 10 minutes at high pressure.

Let the steam release naturally for 10 minutes, then turn the valve to Venting to quick-release any residual steam. Carefully remove the lid and use tongs to transfer the chicken to a plate. When it is cool enough to handle, break it into bite-size pieces. Press the Cancel button.

Press the Sauté button, add the coconut milk, and bring to a rolling simmer. Cook until the sauce starts to thicken, about 5 minutes. Add the green beans, bell pepper, and basil leaves and cook for 10 minutes. Press the Cancel button to reset the program. Add the lime juice and taste for seasoning. Return the chicken to the pot and stir to combine. Remove and discard the lime leaves.

Serve over white rice and top with green onions, cilantro, and basil.

1 stalk lemongrass, tough outer leaves removed

½ lb (225 g) green beans

1 red bell pepper, seeded

2 green Thai chiles

2 small (or 1 large) shallots

4 cloves garlic

2-inch (5-cm) piece fresh ginger, peeled

2 lb (1 kg) boneless, skinless chicken thighs

Kosher salt

2 tablespoons canola oil

2 tablespoons Thai green curry paste

1 cup (240 ml) chicken stock (page 42 or store-bought)

3 tablespoons fish sauce

8 Thai lime leaves

2 cans (13.5 oz/400 ml each) coconut milk

Handful of Thai basil leaves

Juice of 2 limes

FOR SERVING
Steamed white rice (page 44)

Thinly sliced green onions, fresh cilantro leaves, and fresh Thai basil leaves

"Thanksgiving" Dinner

For this year-round riff on Thanksgiving dinner, you can save time by cooking the meat and stuffing together. The stuffing steams well, and quickly, but definitely benefits from baking for a few minutes in the oven at the end to give it a nice golden brown color and crunch (see Bonus Step).

SERVES 4

To make the stuffing, preheat the oven to 425°F (220°C). Grease a 1½-qt (1.5-L) round ceramic baking dish with butter and set aside.

Place the bread cubes on a baking sheet and bake until crisp but not yet browned, 10–15 minutes. Remove from the oven and transfer to a large bowl.

Select Sauté on the Instant Pot® and melt the 2 tablespoons butter. Add the celery, shallots, ½ teaspoon salt, and ¼ teaspoon pepper and cook, stirring often, until softened, about 3 minutes. Add the garlic and cook until fragrant, about 1 minute. Add the wine and cook until almost all of it has evaporated, about 1 minute. Press the Cancel button to reset the program. Transfer the celery mixture to the bread cube bowl. Add the eggs, parsley, and ¼ teaspoon salt and toss to combine. Add 1 cup (240 ml) of the stock and toss to combine (there should be no liquid left at the bottom of the bowl). Transfer the stuffing to the prepared baking dish, and cover with aluminum foil.

Season the turkey with salt and pepper. Select Sauté on the Instant Pot® and heat the oil. Add the turkey and brown evenly on both sides, 6–8 minutes. Transfer to a plate. Add the remaining 2 cups (480 ml) of stock and bring to a simmer, stirring occasionally with a wooden spoon to scrape up any browned bits. Return the turkey to the pot, skin side up, and nestle it in so it fits in one layer. Press the Cancel button to reset the program.

FOR THE STUFFING

2 tablespoons unsalted butter, plus more for greasing

¾ lb (340 g) dry white country bread, cut into 1-inch (2.5-cm) cubes

2 ribs celery, sliced

2 shallots, minced

Kosher salt and freshly ground black pepper

2 cloves garlic, minced

¼ cup (60 ml) white wine

2 large eggs, lightly beaten

¼ cup (7 g) chopped fresh flat-leaf parsley

3 cups (700 ml) chicken stock (page 42 or store-bought)

2 lb (1 kg) bone-in, skin-on turkey or chicken breasts

1 tablespoon canola oil

Creamy Mashed Potatoes (page 40), for serving (optional)

Turkey breasts can be hard to find, but bone-in, skin-on chicken breasts work just as well here. If you have homemade turkey stock on hand, use that in place of the chicken stock. To truly make this a feast, serve it all with a big bowl of mashed potatoes mixed with your favorite flavorings (see page 40).

Place the steam rack on top of the turkey, then place the baking dish on top of the steam rack. (Everything will fit snugly into the pot.) Lock the lid in place and turn the valve to Sealing. Press the Pressure Cook button and set the cook time for 12 minutes at high pressure.

Turn the valve to Venting to quick-release the steam. Remove the lid and, using the steam rack handles, lift out the baking dish. Transfer to a cooling rack, remove the foil, and let cool slightly.

Serve the turkey and stuffing right away, along with creamy mashed potatoes, if desired.

BONUS STEP *After removing it from the pot, bake the stuffing in a preheated 450°F (230°C) oven, uncovered, until golden brown, 10–12 minutes. The crispy top will complement the moist center, creating a perfect texture in every bite.*

TIP *If you'd like to cook more chicken at one time, or if your chicken breasts are too big to fit into one layer in the pot, you can cook the chicken and stuffing separately, each for 12 minutes at high pressure, ensuring that there are at least 2 cups (475 ml) of liquid in the pot for each round. Once the pot is hot, it comes up to pressure much quicker than when it is cold, so the second round of cooking will go quickly.*

Soy-Glazed Salmon with Ginger

Healthy and light, salmon fillets are a breeze to cook in an Instant Pot—and won't leave a fishy smell in your kitchen. Marinating them in a zesty mix of soy sauce, ginger, and lime both tenderizes and flavors the fish, and a sprinkling of toasted sesame seeds imparts a crunchy nuttiness to the finished dish.

SERVES 4

In a small bowl or measuring cup, whisk together the soy sauce, lime zest and juice, ginger, and brown sugar. Place the salmon fillets in a shallow pan or baking dish and pour the marinade over the top. Cover with plastic wrap and marinate in the refrigerator for at least 30 minutes and up to 2 hours.

Transfer the salmon to the Instant Pot®, skin side up, and pour the remaining marinade over the fish. Lock the lid in place and turn the valve to Sealing. Press the Pressure Cook button and set the cook time for 1 minute (for rare salmon) or 2 minutes (for medium salmon) at low pressure.

Let the steam release naturally for 5 minutes, then turn the valve to Venting to quick-release any residual steam. Carefully remove the lid and use tongs to transfer the salmon to a serving platter. Press the Cancel button to reset the program.

Press the Sauté button and simmer the cooking liquid until it has thickened, 3-4 minutes. To serve, spoon over the salmon and top with sesame seeds. Serve rice alongside.

¼ cup (60 ml) soy sauce

Finely grated zest of 1 lime

Juice of 2 limes

2 tablespoons peeled and grated fresh ginger

2 tablespoons firmly packed brown sugar

4 salmon fillets with skin, about 6 oz (180 g) each

Toasted sesame seeds, for serving

Steamed white or brown rice (pages 44–45), for serving

BONUS STEP *To make this dish into a meal, add 1 tablespoon olive oil, 2 cups (150 g) sliced bok choy or other firm green vegetable, and a splash of water to the hot pot after the sauce is spooned over the salmon and cook in Sauté mode until tender, about 3 minutes.*

Indian Fish Curry

Sometimes a simple blend of spices and a nice piece of fish are all you need for a delectable dinner. The sauce for this dish is on the thinner side, but you can use the sauté step at the end to reduce it to your desired consistency. Basmati rice is the perfect vehicle for the flavors in the curry.

SERVES 6

Select Sauté on the Instant Pot® and heat the oil. Add the onion and cook, stirring occasionally, until starting to brown, 5–7 minutes. Add the garlic, chiles, ginger, cumin, coriander, and turmeric, stir to combine, and cook until blended, about 1 minute. Add the tomatoes, sugar, and 1 teaspoon salt, and cook until blended, about 1 minute. Add the water and bring to a boil, stirring occasionally with a wooden spoon to scrape up any browned bits. Press the Cancel button to reset the program.

Lock the lid in place and turn the valve to Sealing. Press the Pressure Cook button and set the cook time for 10 minutes at high pressure.

Let the steam release naturally. Carefully remove the lid and press the Sauté button. Bring to a simmer and cook until the sauce is starting to thicken, 8–10 minutes. Add the fish and cook until opaque and cooked through, 3–5 minutes. Taste and add more salt, if needed.

To serve, spoon the fish and sauce over rice and sprinkle with cilantro.

¼ cup (60 ml) canola oil

1 yellow onion, chopped

2 cloves garlic, minced

2 small hot green chiles, seeded and minced

1-inch (2.5-cm) piece fresh ginger, peeled and grated

1 tablespoon ground cumin

2 teaspoons ground coriander

1 tablespoon ground turmeric

2 tomatoes, seeded and chopped

1 tablespoon granulated or coconut sugar

Kosher salt

1½ cups (350 ml) water

2 lb (1 kg) firm white fish, such as cod or halibut, cut into 2-inch (5-cm) pieces

Steamed white rice (page 44), for serving

Chopped fresh cilantro leaves, for serving

Seafood Paella

This Spanish classic is amazing on its own, but to spice it up a bit, add some chorizo. Before you cook the onion, sauté 1 lb (450 g) cured, sliced Spanish chorizo in 2 tablespoons olive oil until lightly browned, about 4 minutes. Transfer to a plate and return it to the pot when you add the clams.

SERVES 6–8

Select Sauté on the Instant Pot® and heat the oil. Add the onion and garlic and cook, stirring occasionally, until the onion is softened, about 3 minutes. Season with salt and pepper, then add the smoked paprika, sweet paprika, granulated garlic, and saffron. Cook, stirring often, until the onion is well coated with the spices, about 3 minutes. Pour in the wine and bring to a simmer, stirring occasionally with a wooden spoon to scrape up any browned bits. Add the tomatoes, rice, 4 cups (1 L) of the stock, and the clams, discarding any clams that fail to close to the touch. Press the Cancel button to reset the program.

Lock the lid in place and turn the valve to Sealing. Press the Pressure Cook button and set the cook time for 8 minutes at high pressure.

Turn the valve to Venting to quick-release the steam. Carefully remove the lid, and press the Cancel button to reset the program. Select Sauté and add the remaining ½ cup (120 ml) stock, the shrimp, and the peas and cook, stirring occasionally, until the shrimp are opaque throughout and the peas are heated through, about 3 minutes.

Divide the paella among individual bowls, discarding any clams that failed to open. Top with parsley and a squeeze of lemon juice and serve.

2 tablespoons olive oil

1 yellow onion, diced

3 cloves garlic, minced

Kosher salt and freshly ground black pepper

2 teaspoons smoked paprika

1 teaspoon sweet paprika

½ teaspoon granulated garlic

½ teaspoon saffron threads

½ cup (120 ml) dry white wine

1 can (14.5 oz/410 g) crushed tomatoes

2 cups (400 g) basmati rice

4½ cups (1 L plus 120 ml) chicken stock (page 42 or store-bought)

1 lb (450 g) littleneck or other small clams

¾ lb (340 g) large shrimp, peeled and deveined

1½ cups (175 g) frozen peas

Chopped fresh flat-leaf parsley and lemon wedges, for serving

Shells are an iconic pasta for this classic comfort food, but little diners might like smaller shapes like elbow macaroni or ditalini.

Three-Cheese Mac 'n' Cheese

This is definitely an adult mac 'n' cheese. The aromatic blend of cheeses creates a tangy, gooey, creamy meal. For a milder flavor, use all Cheddar cheese and leave out the dry mustard. The bread crumbs come together quickly while the pasta is cooking, and lend a just-from-the-oven finish.

SERVES 6–8

In the Instant Pot®, combine the shells, water, 1½ cups (350 ml) of the cream, 4 tablespoons (60 g) of the butter, and the mustard. Season with 1 teaspoon salt and ½ teaspoon pepper. Give the mixture a stir, then lock the lid in place and turn the valve to Sealing. Press the Pressure Cook button and set the cook time for 7 minutes at high pressure.

While the pasta cooks, make the bread crumbs, if using. In a frying pan over medium heat, heat the oil. Add the bread crumbs and parsley, season with salt and pepper, and cook, stirring constantly, until the crumbs are well toasted, about 3 minutes. Remove from the heat.

Let the steam release naturally for 10 minutes, then turn the valve to Venting to quick-release any residual steam. Carefully remove the lid, add the cheeses, the remaining ½ cup (120 ml) cream, and the remaining 2 tablespoons (30 g) butter, and stir to mix well. Taste and adjust the seasoning, if needed.

Divide among individual bowls, top with the herbed bread crumbs, if using, and freshly ground black pepper, and serve.

1 lb (450 g) medium shells or any short dried pasta

2½ cups (600 ml) water

2 cups (475 ml) heavy cream

6 tablespoons (90 g) unsalted butter

2 teaspoons dry mustard

Kosher salt and freshly ground black pepper

1 cup (115 g) shredded Gruyère cheese

1 cup (115 g) shredded white Cheddar cheese

1 cup (115 g) shredded Fontina cheese

HERBED BREAD CRUMBS (OPTIONAL)

2 tablespoons olive oil

1 cup (100 g) fresh or fine dried bread crumbs, or panko

2 tablespoons chopped fresh flat-leaf parsley

Stuffed Artichokes

Fresh artichokes are at their peak in spring, so take advantage of their mild flavor and unique texture when they're in season by adding a savory stuffing to the center. Serve them as a simple, satisfying lunch or brunch, or pair them with a Potato, Prosciutto & White Cheddar Frittata (page 30) for dinner.

SERVES 4

In a food processor, process the bread until fine crumbs form.

Select Sauté on the Instant Pot® and heat the oil. Add the bread crumbs and cook, stirring occasionally, until golden brown, about 6 minutes. Transfer the crumbs to a bowl and stir in the garlic and lemon zest. Season with salt and pepper and set aside. (This step can also be done in a large frying pan over medium heat on the stove, if preferred.) Using tongs to hold a paper towel, wipe out the pot.

Add the pancetta to the pot and cook, stirring occasionally, until crispy, about 6 minutes. Add to the bread crumb mixture and stir to combine. Press the Cancel button to reset the program.

Working with 1 artichoke at a time, cut off the stem flush with the bottom and discard, then cut 1 inch (2.5 cm) off the top. Using scissors, trim away the thorny tips of the remaining leaves. Using a spoon (serrated if possible), scoop out the choke from the center. Season the insides of the artichokes with salt and pepper. Divide the bread crumb mixture evenly among the artichokes, packing it firmly into the center where the choke was removed. Sprinkle the cheese on top of the filling, dividing it evenly.

Add the wine and water to the pot and insert the steam rack. Place the artichokes, filling side up, on the steam rack. Lock the lid in place and turn the valve to Sealing. Press the Pressure Cook button and set the cook time for 10 minutes at high pressure.

Let the steam release naturally, and carefully remove the lid. Transfer the artichokes to a serving platter and serve warm.

2 cups (80 g) country bread pieces, crusts removed

¾ cup (180 ml) olive oil

3 cloves garlic, minced

2 teaspoons grated lemon zest

Kosher salt and freshly ground black pepper

¼ lb (4 oz/115 g) pancetta, chopped

4 large artichokes

½ cup (60 g) grated Parmesan cheese

½ cup (120 ml) white wine

2½ cups (600 ml) water

Spaghetti Squash

This hard-shelled yellow squash is harvested in the fall and is readily available throughout winter and spring. As the name indicates, its flesh falls away from the shell after cooking in strands like spaghetti. A healthful alternative to pasta, it pairs perfectly with Meatballs & Tomato Sauce (page 58).

SERVES 4–6

Pour the water into the Instant Pot® and insert the steam rack. Place the squash halves, cut side down, in a steamer basket and set it on the steam rack. Lock the lid in place and turn the valve to Sealing. Press the Pressure Cook button and set the cook time for 4–6 minutes at high pressure (about 2 minutes per pound/500 g).

Let the steam release naturally for 5 minutes, then turn the valve to Venting to quick-release any residual steam. Carefully remove the lid and transfer the squash to a cutting board. Gently run a fork along the inside of the squash to scrape the flesh free from the skin, and transfer the strands to a bowl. Drizzle the squash with oil and season with salt and pepper. Serve warm with your favorite sauce.

3 cups (700 ml) water

1 medium spaghetti squash (2–3 lb/1–1.5 kg), halved crosswise and seeded

Olive oil, for drizzling

Kosher salt and freshly ground black pepper

TIP *Alternatively, skip the olive oil and serve the spaghetti squash simply with butter and grated Parmesan cheese, seasoned with a little salt and few grinds of pepper.*

Zesty Wild Rice Salad

This blend of hearty rice, crunchy toppings, and a refreshing vinaigrette is wonderful as a main dish at an outdoor picnic or as a side dish paired with ribs (page 72) or salmon (page 90). Pack leftovers for lunch or a quick meal on the go.

SERVES 6

Rinse the rice in a sieve under cold running water until the water runs clear; shake the sieve to remove excess water.

In the Instant Pot®, combine the drained rice, water, and 1 teaspoon salt. Lock the lid in place and turn the valve to Sealing. Press the Pressure Cook button and set the cook time for 30 minutes at high pressure.

Let the steam release naturally for 10 minutes, then turn the valve to Venting to quick-release any residual steam. Carefully remove the lid. Fluff the rice with a fork.

In a large bowl, combine the rice, bell pepper, green onions, pomegranate seeds, and almonds. In a small bowl, whisk together the vinegar, soy sauce, and ginger. Slowly whisk in the oil to make a dressing. Season to taste with salt and pepper. Pour the dressing over the salad, mix well, and serve.

TIP *To pack this salad for lunch, put the dressing in a separate container and toss everything together when ready to serve.*

1½ cups (240 g) wild rice

4½ cups (1.1 L) water

Kosher salt and freshly ground black pepper

1 large red bell pepper, seeded and diced

2 green onions, thinly sliced

½ cup (80 g) pomegranate seeds

¾ cup (70 g) toasted sliced almonds

3 tablespoons apple cider vinegar

1½ teaspoons soy sauce

½ teaspoon peeled and grated fresh ginger

5 tablespoons (75 ml) olive oil

Risotto Two Ways

Risotto is a blank canvas for a myriad of flavor and texture combinations. Parmesan cheese and lemon is a classic, while goat cheese and spinach is a bit unexpected. With either option, the brilliance of this method is that it eliminates the need for the constant adding and stirring of stock into the rice that often puts people off from making it in the first place.

SERVES 4

Select Sauté on the Instant Pot® and heat the oil. Add the onion and garlic and cook, stirring occasionally, until softened, about 3 minutes. Add the rice and cook, stirring occasionally, until translucent with a white dot in the center, about 3 minutes. Add the wine and bring to a simmer, stirring occasionally with a wooden spoon to scrape up any browned bits. Cook until the wine has reduced slightly, then stir in the stock. Press the Cancel button to reset the program.

Lock the lid in place and turn the valve to Sealing. Press the Pressure Cook button and set the cook time for 7 minutes at high pressure.

Let the steam release naturally, then carefully remove the lid.

For Parmesan & Lemon Risotto, stir the Parmesan and butter into the risotto and season with salt and pepper. Transfer to a serving platter or divide among 4 bowls. Top with the lemon zest and basil and serve right away.

For Spinach & Goat Cheese Risotto, press the Cancel button to reset the program. Select Sauté and stir in the spinach and goat cheese. Cook until the spinach is wilted, about 3 minutes. Stir in the butter and season with salt and pepper. Transfer to a serving platter or divide among 4 bowls and serve right away.

2 tablespoons olive oil

1 yellow onion, diced

2 cloves garlic, minced

2 cups (400 g) Arborio rice

½ cup (120 ml) white wine

4 cups (1 L) vegetable or chicken stock (pages 42–43 or store-bought)

Kosher salt and freshly ground black pepper

STIR-INS FOR PARMESAN & LEMON RISOTTO
½ cup (60 g) grated Parmesan cheese; 1 tablespoon butter; 2 teaspoons grated lemon zest; and ¼ cup (15 g) slivered fresh basil

STIR-INS FOR SPINACH & GOAT CHEESE RISOTTO
2 cups (60 g) baby spinach leaves; ¼ lb (4 oz/115 g) crumbled goat cheese; and 1 tablespoon butter

Vegetable Ragout

The magic of this dish is that everything (except the delicate peas) goes into the pot at once and cooks together quickly for a fresh, healthy sauce that pairs wonderfully with a bowl of creamy polenta. Other hearty vegetables will work here, too, such as cauliflower florets. Just be sure to use firm veggies that can stand up to the pressure.

SERVES 6

Add all of the ingredients except for the peas to the Instant Pot®, along with 1 teaspoon salt and ½ teaspoon pepper, and toss to coat. Lock the lid in place and turn the valve to Sealing. Press the Pressure Cook button and set the cook time for 7 minutes at high pressure.

Let the steam release naturally for 10 minutes, then turn the valve to Venting to quick-release any residual steam. Carefully remove the lid, then remove and discard the thyme springs. Press the Cancel button to reset the program.

Select Sauté and add the peas. Simmer until the peas are cooked through, about 3 minutes. Taste and adjust the seasoning with salt and pepper, if needed.

Serve over bowls of warm polenta, and sprinkle with herbs.

2 leeks, white and pale green parts, halved lengthwise and cut crosswise into ½-inch (12-mm) slices

1 can (14 oz) artichoke hearts, drained (or 1 package frozen artichoke hearts, thawed)

1 cup (180 g) grape or cherry tomatoes

10 cloves garlic, smashed

½ yellow onion, chopped

¼ cup (60 ml) white wine

¼ cup (60 ml) vegetable or chicken stock (pages 42–43 or store-bought)

2 tablespoons olive oil

1 tablespoon white wine vinegar

2 sprigs fresh thyme

Kosher salt and freshly ground black pepper

1½ cups (175 g) fresh or thawed frozen English peas

Polenta (page 41), for serving

Chopped fresh basil and/or mint leaves, for serving

Chicken-Tortilla Soup (page 112)

SOUPS & STEWS

Tom Kha Gai Soup

A robust blend of coconut milk, lemongrass, red chiles, Thai lime leaves, and galangal (a root in the ginger family) comes together for a delectable yet easy-to-make Thai soup. Bruising the lemongrass is key to unlocking its flavor.

SERVES 6

To bruise the lemongrass, use the flat side of your knife and firmly push down on the inner stalk until it splits open. Then cut the stalks into 3-inch (7.5-cm) pieces.

Combine all the ingredients except the coconut sugar, lime juice, and cilantro leaves in the Instant Pot®. Lock the lid in place and turn the valve to Sealing. Press the Soup button and set the cook time for 20 minutes at high pressure.

Let the steam release naturally, or for at least 15 minutes, before turning the valve to Venting to quick-release any residual steam. Carefully remove the lid and remove and discard the lime leaves, lemongrass, and galangal. Shred the chicken into bite-size pieces using two forks. Add the coconut sugar and lime juice and stir to combine.

To serve, ladle into bowls and top with cilantro, along with lime wedges.

2 stalks lemongrass, tough outer leaves removed

1 lb (450 g) boneless, skinless chicken thighs

2-inch (5-cm) piece galangal or fresh ginger, peeled and thickly sliced

1 small onion, sliced

2–4 red Thai chiles (depending on heat desired), bruised

8 oz (250 g) white button mushrooms, quartered

8 Thai lime leaves

2 cans (13.5 oz/400 ml each) full-fat coconut milk

1 cup (240 ml) chicken stock (page 42 or store-bought)

3 tablespoons fish sauce

1 tablespoon coconut sugar

Juice of 1 lime

Fresh cilantro leaves or sprigs, for serving

Lime wedges, for serving

Seek out lemongrass, Thai lime leaves, and Thai chiles, as they are all essential in creating the authentic flavors of this effortless soup.

Curried Cauliflower Soup

This soup is deceptive: it's smooth and creamy but dairy free. Madras curry originates from southern India, and the powder is usually a bit spicier than other curry powders. If you have trouble finding it, you can substitute regular curry powder and add a dash of cayenne pepper for more heat.

SERVES 6

Select Sauté on the Instant Pot® and melt the butter. Add the onion and cook until softened, about 3 minutes. Add the stock, potatoes, cauliflower, and ½ teaspoon salt and stir to combine. Press the Cancel button to reset the program.

Lock the lid in place and turn the valve to Sealing. Press the Pressure Cook button and set the cook time for 5 minutes at high pressure.

Let the steam release naturally. Stir the curry powder into the soup. Press the Cancel button to reset the program.

Let the soup stand until no longer steaming hot, then purée it in batches in a blender (or with an immersion blender directly in the pot) until very smooth. Season to taste with salt. Ladle into bowls, top with the croutons, if using, and serve right away.

1 tablespoon unsalted butter

1 yellow onion, chopped

5 cups (1.25 L) vegetable or chicken stock (pages 42–43 or store-bought)

½ lb (225 g) Yukon gold potatoes, peeled and cut into 1-inch (2.5-cm) pieces

1 medium head cauliflower, trimmed and cut into 1-inch (2.5-cm) pieces

Kosher salt

1½ teaspoons Madras curry powder

Spicy Croutons (recipe follows), for garnish (optional)

MAKES ABOUT 2 CUPS (120 G)

SPICY CROUTONS

Preheat the oven to 425°F (220°C). Cut the bread into ½-inch (12-mm) cubes and place in a large bowl. Melt the butter and pour it over the bread cubes. In a small bowl, stir together the paprika, salt, cayenne, and cumin. Sprinkle the spices over the bread cubes and toss to combine. Spread the bread on a baking sheet lined with aluminum foil and bake until crisp, about 10 minutes. Let cool and use right away.

4 oz (115 g) white country bread

2 tablespoons unsalted butter

1 teaspoon paprika

½ teaspoon Kosher salt

¼ teaspoon cayenne pepper

¼ teaspoon ground cumin

Black Lentil & Vegetable Dahl

There are so many variations of the beloved Indian dish dahl, from the type of lentils used to the spice combinations. This version features black lentils, since they stand up to pressure better than softer red lentils. Don't skip the butter at the end—a bit luxurious, it really brings the dish to the next level.

SERVES 4–6

In a small bowl, combine the garlic, ginger, coriander, cumin, cayenne, and turmeric and stir to combine. Set aside.

Select Sauté on the Instant Pot® and heat 1 tablespoon of the oil. Add the cauliflower and ½ teaspoon salt and cook for 1 minute. Add the 2 tablespoons water and cook, stirring occasionally, until the cauliflower begins to soften, about 5 minutes. Transfer to a plate with a slotted spoon and set aside.

Heat the remaining 2 tablespoons oil, add the onion, and cook, stirring occasionally, until softened, about 3 minutes. Add the spice mixture, stir to combine, and cook until blended, about 1 minute. Add the tomatoes and cook until blended, about 1 minute. Press the Cancel button to reset the program.

Add the lentils, the 4 cups (1 L) water, and 1 teaspoon salt to the pot and stir to combine. Lock the lid in place and turn the valve to Sealing. Press the Pressure Cook button and set the cook time for 15 minutes at high pressure.

Let the steam release naturally. Carefully remove the lid, return the cauliflower to the pot, and stir to combine. Stir in the butter. Taste and add more salt, if needed.

Spoon the dahl over rice, sprinkle with cilantro, and serve with a plate of warm naan alongside.

3 cloves garlic, minced

1-inch (2.5-cm) piece of fresh ginger, peeled and grated

1 tablespoon ground coriander

1 teaspoon ground cumin

¼ teaspoon cayenne pepper

¼ teaspoon ground turmeric

3 tablespoons grapeseed or coconut oil

2 cups (120 g) bite-size cauliflower florets

Kosher salt

4 cups (1 L) water plus 2 tablespoons

1 small yellow onion, diced

1 cup (240 ml) puréed or finely chopped tomatoes

1 cup (200 g) black lentils

2 tablespoons unsalted butter

Steamed rice (page 44), chopped fresh cilantro leaves, and naan bread, for serving

Fully Loaded Baked Potato Soup

Everyone knows that the best bites of a baked potato are the ones with all the toppings. With a double dose of sour cream—in the soup as well as drizzled on top—and a full suite of creamy Cheddar cheese, crispy bacon, and zesty green onions, you'll never want for more of the good stuff in this soup.

SERVES 6

Select Sauté on the Instant Pot® and melt the butter. Add the onion and cook until tender and translucent, about 5 minutes. Add the garlic and cook until fragrant, 1 minute. Add the stock and bring to a simmer, stirring occasionally with a wooden spoon to scrape up any browned bits. Press the Cancel button to reset the program.

Add the potatoes, 1 teaspoon salt, and ½ teaspoon pepper. Lock the lid in place and turn the valve to Sealing. Press the Pressure Cook button and set the cook time for 25 minutes at high pressure.

Let the steam release naturally, or for at least 15 minutes, before turning the valve to Venting to quick-release any residual steam. Carefully remove the lid. Use an immersion blender to blend the potato mixture until smooth. (Alternatively, transfer the potato mixture to a blender and blend until smooth, working in batches if necessary.) While the soup is still hot, stir or blend in the 1 cup (225 g) sour cream until smooth. Stir in the heavy cream, if using. Taste and adjust the seasoning as needed.

Ladle into bowls and top with crumbled bacon, green onions, cheese, and a dollop of sour cream. Sprinkle with pepper and serve right away.

1 tablespoon unsalted butter

1 yellow onion, diced

4–5 cloves garlic, minced

4 cups (1 L) chicken stock (page 42 or store-bought)

2 lb (1 kg) russet potatoes, peeled and cut into 1-inch (2.5-cm) cubes

Kosher salt and freshly ground black pepper

1 cup (225 g) sour cream, plus more for serving

¼ cup (60 ml) heavy cream (optional)

2–3 slices (3 oz/90 g) thick-cut bacon, cooked and crumbled, for serving

Sliced green onions, for serving

Shredded sharp Cheddar cheese, for serving

Pork Ramen

A beautiful bowl of Japanese ramen soup is a blank canvas for your favorite flavorings and toppings. Fresh ramen noodles, found in the refrigerated section of well-stocked grocery stores, will taste best and be most authentic here, but you can use dried noodles as well.

SERVES 6

Season the pork generously with salt. Select Sauté on the Instant Pot® and heat the oil. Working in batches, add the pork and brown evenly on all sides, about 5 minutes per side. Transfer to a plate as browned. Using tongs to hold a paper towel, wipe out all but 2 tablespoons of the fat from the pot. Add the onion and cook, stirring occasionally with a wooden spoon and scraping up any browned bits, until softened, about 3 minutes. Add the garlic and ginger and cook until fragrant, about 1 minute. Add 1 cup (240 ml) of the stock and cook for 1 minute. Press the Cancel button to reset the program.

Add the leek, mushrooms, and remaining 7 cups (1.75 L) stock and stir. Return the pork to the pot. Lock the lid in place and turn the valve to Sealing. Press the Pressure Cook button and set the cook time for 45 minutes at high pressure.

Prepare the noodles according to the package directions; set aside.

Let the steam release naturally for 20 minutes, then turn the valve to Venting to quick-release any residual steam. Carefully remove the lid and transfer the pork to a plate. When the pork is cool enough to handle, shred it into bite-size pieces. Pour the broth through a fine-mesh sieve into a large bowl. Discard the solids, reserving the mushroom slices, if desired. Skim or strain the fat from the broth. Add the soy sauce. Taste and add more soy sauce, if desired.

Divide the noodles among 6 bowls, ladle the broth on top, and add desired toppings. Serve with sesame and/or chile oil alongside.

2 lb (1 kg) boneless pork shoulder, cut into 3 pieces

Kosher salt

1 tablespoon canola oil

1 yellow onion, chopped

6 cloves garlic, chopped

2-inch (5-cm) piece of fresh ginger, peeled and chopped

8 cups (2 L) chicken stock (page 42 or store-bought)

1 leek, white and light green parts, sliced crosswise

¼ lb (115 g) cremini or white button mushrooms, sliced

1½ lb (680 g) fresh or dried ramen noodles

1 tablespoon soy sauce, plus more as needed

FOR SERVING

Peeled and halved soft-boiled eggs (page 32), sliced green onions, sesame seeds, roasted nori seaweed strips, bok choy, sliced napa cabbage, and/ or shiitake mushrooms, plus sesame and/or chile oil

Chicken Pho

Traditionally eaten for breakfast in Vietnam, this heartwarming soup is all about the robust broth. Serve piping-hot bowls with a plate of garnishes alongside and add a little of each item as you eat, so that the herbs stay bright and fragrant and the bean sprouts maintain their crispness.

SERVES 4–6

Season the chicken generously with salt. Select Sauté on the Instant Pot® and heat the oil. Working in batches, brown the chicken on both sides, about 3 minutes per side. Transfer to a plate as browned. Using tongs to hold a paper towel, wipe out all but 2 tablespoons of the fat from the pot. Add the yellow onions and ginger and cook, stirring occasionally, until softened and just starting to brown, 3–5 minutes. Press the Cancel button to reset the program.

To bruise the lemongrass, use the flat side of your knife and firmly push down on the inner stalk until it splits open. Cut the stalks into 3-inch (7.5-cm) pieces. Return the chicken to the pot. Add the lemongrass, cilantro, green onions, fish sauce, brown sugar, and water and stir. Lock the lid in place and turn the valve to Sealing. Press the Pressure Cook button and set the cook time for 30 minutes at high pressure.

Let the steam release naturally for 15 minutes, then turn the valve to Venting to quick-release any residual steam. Carefully remove the lid and transfer the chicken to a cutting board. When it's cool enough to handle, remove the meat, discarding the skin and bones, and shred into bite-size pieces. Pour the broth through a fine-mesh sieve into a large bowl. Discard the solids. Press the Cancel button to reset the program.

Soften the rice noodles in hot water and drain; set aside. Season the broth with fish sauce as desired. Return the broth to the Instant Pot®, press the Sauté button, and bring to a boil. Add the bok choy and simmer for 2 minutes. Add the chicken and the rice noodles and simmer until heated through, about 3 minutes.

Arrange the garnishes on a platter. Ladle the soup into bowls and serve right away with the garnishes alongside.

3 lb (1.5 kg) bone-in, skin-on whole chicken legs

Kosher salt

1 tablespoon canola oil

2 yellow onions, quartered

3-inch (7.5-cm) piece fresh ginger, peeled and cut into thin rounds

3 stalks lemongrass, tough outer leaves removed

6 fresh cilantro sprigs

3 green onions, white and pale green parts, cut into 3-inch (7.5-cm) pieces

¼ cup (60 ml) fish sauce, plus more as needed

2 tablespoons firmly packed light brown sugar

8 cups (2 L) water

1 package (8 oz/225 g) dried rice noodles

2 heads baby bok choy, thinly sliced

FOR SERVING
Sliced green onions, mung bean sprouts, fresh cilantro leaves, fresh basil or Thai basil leaves, sliced jalapeño chiles, and/or lime wedges

Chicken-Tortilla Soup

Warm, cozy, and comforting, this Mexican staple is seriously addictive. The spicy, smoky flavor of the broth is brought to life with an array of creamy, crispy, and salty toppings. Keep a stash of soup in your freezer for a quick dinner any night of the week.

SERVES 6

Put the chiles in a small heatproof bowl, cover with boiling water, and let soak for 10 minutes. Drain and discard the liquid.

In a blender or food processor, combine the chiles, tomatoes, onion, garlic, and 1 cup (240 ml) of the stock. Blend until smooth.

Select Sauté on the Instant Pot® and heat the oil. Working in batches, brown the chicken on both sides, about 3 minutes per side. Transfer to a plate as browned. Press the Cancel button to reset the program.

Add the chile purée, cumin, oregano, 1 teaspoon salt, and ½ teaspoon pepper to the pot and stir to combine. Return the chicken to the pot and add the remaining 5 cups (1.25 L) stock and the bay leaves. Lock the lid in place and turn the valve to Sealing. Press the Soup button and set the cook time for 20 minutes at high pressure.

Let the steam release naturally, or for at least 15 minutes, before turning the valve to Venting to quick-release any residual steam. Carefully remove the lid and discard the bay leaves. Using two forks, shred the chicken. Taste and adjust the seasoning as needed. Discard the bay leaves.

Ladle the soup into bowls and top with avocado slices, cheese, tortilla chips, cilantro, and a drizzle of sour cream. Serve right away.

3 dried ancho chiles, stemmed, seeded, and torn into pieces

1 can (14.5 oz/410 g) crushed tomatoes

1 yellow onion, roughly chopped

3 cloves garlic

6 cups (1.5 L) chicken stock (page 42 or store-bought)

2 tablespoons olive oil

2 lb (1 kg) boneless, skinless chicken thighs

1 teaspoon cumin

1 teaspoon dried oregano, preferably Mexican

Kosher salt and freshly ground black pepper

3 bay leaves

FOR SERVING
Avocado slices, crumbled Cotija cheese, crushed tortilla chips, chopped fresh cilantro leaves, and/or sour cream

Dried ancho chiles are almost black in color, but after soaking they transform into a rich mahogany hue.

White Bean Cassoulet with Sausage

Inspired by the traditional French pork and white bean stew, this version features smoked sausage and bacon, along with dried beans that cook in just 40 minutes, no soaking required. A green salad and thick slices of toasted country bread would be the perfect accompaniment.

SERVES 4–6

Select Sauté on the Instant Pot® and add the bacon. Cook until the bacon is browned and most of the fat is rendered, about 5 minutes. Use a slotted spoon to transfer the bacon pieces to a paper towel–lined plate. Add the sausage and cook until starting to brown, about 5 minutes. Transfer the sausage slices to a plate.

Using tongs to hold a paper towel, wipe out all but 2 tablespoons of fat from the pot. Add the onion and carrots and cook until they start to brown, 5–7 minutes. (You can add 1 tablespoon of the wine to the pot now if it has a lot of dark brown bits threatening to burn.) Add the garlic and cook until fragrant, about 1 minute. Add the wine and bring to a simmer, stirring occasionally with a wooden spoon to scrape up any browned bits. Cook until the wine is reduced by almost half, about 2 minutes. Add the stock, brown sugar, mustard, coriander, bay leaf, and a few grindings of pepper, stir, and bring to a simmer. Press the Cancel button to reset the program.

Add the beans, bacon, and sausage to the pot. Lock the lid in place and turn the valve to Sealing. Press the Pressure Cook button and set the cook time for 40 minutes at high pressure.

Let the steam release naturally. Carefully remove the lid and discard the bay leaf. Taste and adjust the seasoning, as needed.

To serve, ladle the stew into bowls and garnish with parsley.

4 slices (about 4 oz/115 g) thick-cut applewood-smoked or other bacon, chopped

1 lb (450 g) fully cooked smoked sausage, cut into slices ½ inch (12 mm) thick

1 yellow onion, diced

2 carrots, peeled and diced

4 cloves garlic, minced

1 cup (240 ml) white wine

2½ cups (600 ml) chicken stock (page 42 or store-bought)

2 tablespoons firmly packed dark brown sugar

1 tablespoon Dijon mustard

¼ teaspoon ground coriander

1 bay leaf

Kosher salt and freshly ground black pepper

1 cup (200 g) dried white beans, such as cannellini or great northern

Chopped fresh flat-leaf parsley, for serving

Texas Beef Chili

Texas-style chili has no beans. It's traditionally a long-simmered dish made with beef stew meat (such as chuck) and a combo of chile peppers and spices, but this version cooks in a fraction of the time. For the most authentic taste, use ground chiles rather than preblended chile powder (see Tip below).

SERVES 4–6

Pat the meat dry with paper towels and season it lightly all over with salt.

Select Sauté on the Instant Pot® and heat 2 tablespoons of the oil. Working in batches, brown the meat evenly, about 8 minutes total. Transfer to a plate as browned. Add the remaining 1 tablespoon oil and the onion and cook until softened, about 3 minutes. Add the garlic and cook until fragrant, about 1 minute. Stir in the chile powder, paprika, cumin, and oregano. Pour in the water, then stir in the tomato paste until blended. Return the meat and any accumulated juices to the pot, then stir to coat the meat with sauce. Press the Cancel button to reset the program.

Lock the lid in place and turn the valve to Sealing. Press the Pressure Cook button and set the cook time for 15 minutes at high pressure.

Let the steam release naturally. Carefully remove the lid and let the chili stand for 5 minutes to settle the flavors.

Ladle the chili into bowls and top each portion with sour cream, cheese, and/or green onions, as desired. Serve right away.

3 lb (1.5 kg) beef chuck, cut into 1-inch (2.5-cm) cubes

Kosher salt

3 tablespoons canola oil

1 yellow onion, chopped

2 cloves garlic, minced

3 tablespoons ancho chile powder, homemade or store-bought

1 tablespoon sweet paprika

2 teaspoons ground cumin

1 teaspoon dried oregano

1½ cups (375 ml) water

½ cup (120 ml) tomato paste

FOR SERVING
Sour cream, grated Cheddar cheese, and/or sliced green onions

TIP *You can make your own ancho chile powder by lightly toasting dried ancho chiles in a dry frying pan over low heat on the stove for a few minutes. When the chiles are cool enough to handle, remove the stems and tear the chiles into pieces. Put the pieces into a spice grinder, clean coffee grinder, or small food processor, and blend until ground.*

Smoky Seafood Chowder

A hearty chowder is as delicious on a warm summer afternoon paired with a glass of rosé as it is on a chilly fall night served with a pint of beer. Tuck in with a slice of crusty bread for the ultimate seafood-lover's meal. If you'd like to leave out the bacon, cook the onion and celery in 2 tablespoons of canola oil instead—keep in mind that the overall flavor will be slightly less smoky and rich but still wonderfully delicious.

SERVES 6

Select Sauté on the Instant Pot® and add the bacon. Cook until the bacon is crispy and almost all the fat has rendered, about 5 minutes. Transfer to a paper towel–lined plate. Add the onion and celery and cook, stirring occasionally with a wooden spoon and scraping up any browned bits, until the vegetables are softened, about 5 minutes. Add ½ cup (120 ml) of the wine and cook for 1 minute. Press the Cancel button to reset the program.

Add the potatoes, bacon, stock, and 1 teaspoon salt to the pot. Lock the lid in place and turn the valve to Sealing. Press the Pressure Cook button and set the cook time for 7 minutes at high pressure.

Meanwhile, arrange the clams in a single layer in a medium sauté pan and pour in the remaining ½ cup (120 ml) wine and the water. Place over medium-low heat, cover, and steam until the clams open, 5–10 minutes. Drain the liquid and discard any clams that failed to open. Set aside.

2 slices (about 2 oz/60 g) thick-cut applewood-smoked bacon, chopped

1 yellow onion, finely chopped

2 ribs celery, sliced

1 cup (240 ml) white wine

1 lb (450 g) Yukon gold potatoes, cut into 1-inch (2.5-cm) pieces

4 cups (1 L) chicken or vegetable stock (pages 42–43 or store-bought)

Kosher salt and freshly ground black pepper

1 lb (450 g) fresh clams

½ cup (120 ml) water

continued on page 118

continued from page 117

Let the steam release naturally for 15 minutes, then turn the valve to Venting to quick-release any residual steam. Press the Cancel button to reset the program. Carefully remove the lid and press the Sauté button. Add the fish and corn and bring the broth to a simmer. Add the cream and simmer until well combined, about 3 minutes. Press the Cancel button to reset the program.

Add the salmon, cooked clams, and shrimp, and let cook in the hot broth until the shrimp are pink, about 1 minute. Taste and adjust the seasoning as needed.

To serve, ladle the chowder into bowls, top with chives and freshly ground black pepper, and accompany with slices of crusty bread.

TIP *This soup is quite literally a melting pot for any fresh seafood flavors. Swap the clams for mussels, or add other tender varieties at the end with the white fish, such as sea or bay scallops.*

You can prepare the soup through the pressure cooking step and freeze it in airtight containers for up to 2 months. Defrost and reheat the soup base in a large pot on the stove, bring to a simmer, then add the white fish, corn, cream, and other seafood and cook as directed above.

1 lb (450 g) thick white fish, such as halibut or cod, skinned and cut into 2-inch (5-cm) pieces

1½ cups (270 g) frozen or fresh corn kernels

¾ cup (180 ml) heavy cream

½ lb (225 g) hot-smoked salmon, skinned and broken into 2-inch (5-cm) pieces

½ lb (225 g) medium shrimp, peeled and deveined

Chopped chives and crusty bread, for serving

All-in-One Beef Stew

Meat, vegetables, and potatoes cook together for an easy, family-friendly one-pot meal. To make it more of a classic French-style stew, add some sliced mushrooms and white pearl onions (thawed if frozen) to the stew when it simmers at the end.

SERVES 6

Pat the meat dry with paper towels and season it with 2 teaspoons salt and 1 teaspoon pepper.

Select Sauté on the Instant Pot® and add the bacon. Cook until the bacon is browned and most of the fat is rendered, about 5 minutes. Use a slotted spoon to transfer the bacon pieces to a paper towel–lined plate.

Add the oil to the pot and, working in batches if needed, brown the beef evenly, about 8 minutes total. Transfer to a plate as browned. Add 1 tablespoon stock and stir with a wooden spoon to scrape up any browned bits. Add the onion and celery and cook until beginning to soften, about 3 minutes. Add the garlic and tomato paste, stir to combine, and cook for about 1 minute. Add the remaining stock and the wine and cook for 1 minute. Press the Cancel button to reset the program.

Return the beef to the pot, add the potatoes, carrots, thyme, bay leaf, and Worcestershire sauce. Lock the lid in place and turn the valve to Sealing. Press the Pressure Cook button and set the cook time for 25 minutes at high pressure.

Let the steam release naturally. Press the Cancel button to reset the program. Remove the lid and press the Sauté button. Bring the stew to a simmer and cook until thickened, 3–5 minutes, depending on desired thickness. Discard the bay leaf and thyme sprigs. Taste and adjust the seasoning as needed.

Ladle the stew into bowls and serve right away.

3 lb (1.5 kg) beef chuck, cut into 2-inch (5-cm) cubes

Kosher salt and freshly ground black pepper

2 slices (about 2 oz/60 g) thick-cut bacon, diced

1 tablespoon canola oil

1 cup (240 ml) beef stock (page 43 or store-bought)

1 yellow onion, chopped

2 ribs celery, sliced

3 cloves garlic, smashed

1 tablespoon tomato paste

1 cup (240 ml) red wine

1 lb (450 g) Yukon gold potatoes, cut into 2-inch (5-cm) pieces

3 carrots, cut into 1½-inch (5-cm) chunks

2 sprigs fresh thyme

1 tablespoon Worcestershire sauce

1 bay leaf

Chocolate Fudge Cake (page 134)

DESSERTS

Candied lemon peel adds an elegant and delicious finish to this dessert—and it's surprisingly simple to make. (see page 124)

Meyer Lemon–Gingersnap Cheesecake

Meyer lemons, which are in season during the winter and early spring, are a lemon-orange hybrid—slightly sweeter and more fragrant than traditional lemons, making them wonderful to bake with. If you have trouble finding them, you can substitute regular lemons. Don't let the rest of the rich ingredients mislead you—the steam helps to create a light and airy cheesecake texture atop a scrumptious no-bake crust. You won't be able to have just one bite.

SERVES 6–8

To make the crust, lightly grease a 7-inch (18-cm) springform pan with butter. In a food processor, pulse the cookies and salt until crumbs form. Add the melted butter and pulse until the crumbs resemble a rough sand texture. Press into the prepared pan and set aside.

To make the cheesecake, in a stand mixer fitted with the paddle attachment, mix the cream cheese, heavy cream, and sugar on medium speed until well combined, about 3 minutes. Add the eggs and mix until combined. Add the lemon zest and juice, vanilla, and salt and mix until combined. Pour over the crust in the springform pan and cover with aluminum foil.

Pour the water into the Instant Pot® and place the springform pan on the steam rack. Using the handles, lower the pan into the pot. Lock the lid in place and turn the valve to Sealing. Press the Pressure Cook button and set the cook time for 35 minutes at high pressure.

Let the steam release naturally for 15 minutes, then turn the valve to Venting to quick-release any residual steam. Carefully remove the lid and, using the steam rack handles, lift out the pan. Transfer to a cooling rack, remove the foil, and let cool completely. Cover with plastic wrap and refrigerate for at least 2 hours or up to overnight.

To serve, remove the pan sides and cut the cake into wedges.

continued on page 124

FOR THE CRUST

5 oz (150 g) gingersnap cookies

Pinch of kosher salt

¼ cup (½ stick/60 g) unsalted butter, melted, plus more for greasing

FOR THE CHEESECAKE

1 lb (450 g) cream cheese, at room temperature

¼ cup (60 ml) heavy cream

¾ cup (115 g) sugar

2 large eggs, at room temperature, lightly beaten

Zest and juice of 1 Meyer lemon

1 teaspoon pure vanilla extract

Pinch of kosher salt

2 cups (475 ml) water

Candied lemon peel, for garnish (optional)

continued from page 123

VARIATIONS

If you leave out the lemon juice and zest from the batter, you have a wonderful base recipe for cheesecake that could take many directions.

- *Replace the lemon with fresh Key lime juice and zest for a new twist on Key lime pie—a perfect match for the gingersnap crust.*

- *Swap the candied lemon peel for fresh, seasonal berries and serve with a big bowl of fresh whipped cream alongside.*

- *When berries are not in season, top plain cheesecake with Mixed Berry Compote (page 137) made from frozen berries.*

BONUS STEP *To make a candied lemon peel garnish, thinly slice the peel of one lemon, place it in a saucepan filled with water, and bring to a boil. Let boil for a few minutes, then drain out the water and set the lemon peel slices aside. In the same saucepan, make a simple syrup by boiling equal parts sugar and water—for this purpose, start with 1½ cups (375 g) sugar and 1½ cups (350 ml) water. Return the lemon peel slices to the pot and simmer for the time that the cheesecake is steaming, about 35 minutes. Turn off the heat and let cool to room temperature. Chill in an airtight container overnight in the fridge, and use to garnish the cheesecake when ready to serve.*

Individual Chocolate Lava Cakes

Each guest at dinner will love getting his or her own little molten chocolate cake for dessert. You can use semisweet or bittersweet (60 to 70 percent cacao) for this recipe, depending on how intense you like your chocolate. Whipped crème fraîche is a twist on traditional whipped cream, but either will work for topping these irresistible treats.

SERVES 4

Lightly grease four 4-oz (120-ml) ramekins with butter, then dust each with about ¾ teaspoon of the sugar.

Fill a saucepan about one-fourth full with water and bring to a steady simmer. Combine the ½ cup (1 stick/115 g) butter and the chocolate in a heatproof bowl, place over (not touching) the simmering water, and heat, stirring occasionally, until the butter and chocolate have melted and are smooth. Remove from the heat, whisk in the 1 cup (200 g) sugar, and then whisk in the eggs, egg yolks, and vanilla until blended. Sift the flour and salt into the chocolate mixture. Using a rubber spatula, fold in the flour just until no streaks remain. Divide the batter evenly among the prepared ramekins and cover each with aluminum foil.

Pour the water into the Instant Pot® and insert the steam rack. Place the ramekins on the rack. Lock the lid in place and turn the valve to Sealing. Press the Pressure Cook button and set the cook time for 9 minutes at high pressure.

Turn the valve to Venting to quick release the steam. Carefully remove the lid and let cool slightly, then remove the ramekins from the pot. Serve the cakes warm, topped with whipped crème fraîche.

½ cup (1 stick/115 g) unsalted butter, plus more for greasing

1 cup (200 g) sugar, plus 1 tablespoon for the ramekins

6 oz (180 g) semisweet or bittersweet chocolate, roughly chopped

2 large eggs, plus 2 large egg yolks

1½ teaspoons pure vanilla extract

6 tablespoons (45 g) all purpose flour

¼ teaspoon kosher salt

2 cups (475 ml) water

Whipped crème fraîche or whipped cream, for serving

You can use any nut butter here, such as almond or cashew, in place of the peanut butter.

Dark Chocolate Pots de Crème with Peanut Butter Swirls

Who doesn't love a rich, creamy bowl of chocolate pudding? Made with dark chocolate, eggs, heavy cream, and milk, this heavenly dessert becomes even more irresistible with the addition of peanut butter swirls. But you could also leave out the peanut butter and top these custards with whipped cream and fresh berries, or just a sprinkle of sea salt and a dollop of crème fraîche.

SERVES 6

In a saucepan over low heat, combine the cream and milk and bring to a simmer. Meanwhile, in a large bowl, whisk together the egg yolks, sugar, and ½ teaspoon salt. Whisk about ¼ cup (60 ml) of the hot cream mixture into the egg yolk mixture. Pour that mixture into the saucepan and continue to whisk rapidly over low heat until combined. Cook, whisking continually, until the mixture has thickened slightly, about 5 minutes. Remove the saucepan from the heat. Add the chocolate chips and whisk until melted. Return the saucepan to the heat and cook, whisking continually, until the mixture has thickened, 5–7 minutes more. Divide evenly among six 4-oz (120-ml) ramekins.

Warm the peanut butter in a microwave-safe bowl for 15 seconds or in a small saucepan over low heat until it is pourable. Drizzle about 1 tablespoon of peanut butter in a swirl on top of each ramekin. Use a butter knife to swirl the peanut butter into the chocolate, if needed. Cover each ramekin with aluminum foil.

1 cup (240 ml) heavy cream

1 cup (240 ml) whole milk

5 large egg yolks

⅓ cup (70 g) sugar

Kosher salt

8 oz (225 g) semisweet chocolate chips

½ cup (115 g) smooth peanut butter

2 cups (475 ml) water

continued on page 128

continued from page 127

Pour the water into the Instant Pot® and insert the steam rack. Place 3 ramekins on the rack in a single layer. Lock the lid in place and turn the valve to Sealing. Press the Pressure Cook button and set the cook time for 6 minutes at high pressure.

Let the steam release naturally for 5 minutes, then turn the valve to Venting to quick-release any residual steam. Carefully remove the lid and remove the ramekins from the pot. Repeat to cook the remaining 3 ramekins.

When all are cooked, let cool to room temperature, cover with plastic wrap, and refrigerate until set, for at least 2 hours or up to 3 days.

VARIATION

Pots de Crème: *If you're not in the mood for peanut butter, leave it out and use the chocolate base as a blank canvas for other flavors. Top each ramekin with a handful of fresh raspberries, blackberries, or sliced strawberries and a swirl of whipped cream, or add a sprinkle of sea salt and a swirl of crème fraîche.*

TIP *To cook all 6 custards at once, place a plate on top of the first 3 ramekins and place the remaining 3 ramekins on top of the plate.*

Cappuccino Crème Brûlée

The combination of espresso and heavy cream creates a luscious cappuccino flavor for this classic French dessert. Steeping the cream with a vanilla bean and its seeds infuses the custard with extra vanilla intensity, but if you don't have one on hand, you can use vanilla extract instead.

SERVES 6

In a saucepan over medium heat, combine the cream, the vanilla bean and its seeds and bring to a simmer. Turn off the heat, cover, and let steep for 15 minutes. Remove the vanilla bean. Add the espresso (and vanilla extract if using it instead of the vanilla bean) and stir to combine.

Meanwhile, in a large bowl, whisk together the egg yolks, granulated sugar, and a pinch of salt. Quickly whisk about ¼ cup (60 ml) of the warm cream mixture into the egg yolk mixture, then whisk in the remaining cream mixture. Pour the mixture through a fine-mesh sieve placed over a large measuring cup or pitcher. Divide evenly among six 4-oz (120-ml) ramekins. Cover each ramekin with aluminum foil.

Pour the water into the Instant Pot® and insert the steam rack. Place 3 ramekins on the steam rack in a single layer. Lock the lid in place and turn the valve to Sealing. Press the Pressure Cook button and set the cook time for 8 minutes at high pressure.

Let the steam release naturally for 5 minutes, then turn the valve to Venting to quick-release any residual steam. Carefully remove the lid and remove the ramekins from the pot. Repeat to cook the remaining 3 ramekins. (To cook all 6 custards at once, place a plate on top of the first 3 ramekins and place the remaining 3 ramekins on top of the plate.)

When all are cooked, let cool to room temperature, cover with plastic wrap, and refrigerate until set, for at least 2 hours or up to 3 days.

Remove the ramekins from the refrigerator about 30 minutes before you are ready to serve them. Preheat the broiler. Place the ramekins on a rimmed baking sheet and sprinkle each with 2 teaspoons turbinado sugar. Broil until the sugar has darkened, 3–5 minutes. Serve right away.

2 cups (475 ml) heavy cream

1 vanilla bean, split and scraped, or 2 teaspoons pure vanilla extract

1 espresso (or 2 tablespoons boiling water mixed with 1 tablespoon instant espresso powder)

5 large egg yolks

⅓ cup (70 g) granulated sugar

Kosher salt

2 cups (475 ml) water

4 tablespoons turbinado sugar

Spiced Apple & Raisin Bread Pudding

The next time you have a loaf of bread lying around going stale, transform it into a luscious, custardy bread pudding layered with spiced apples and sweet raisins. Wonderful on its own, this dessert also welcomes a scoop of vanilla ice cream or a dollop of freshly whipped cream on top.

SERVES 6–8

Grease a 1½-qt (1.5-L) round ceramic baking dish with butter.

In a medium bowl, combine the sugar, cinnamon, and cardamom. Add the apples and toss to coat. In another medium bowl, whisk together the eggs, milk, vanilla, and a pinch of salt.

Arrange one-third of the bread cubes in a single layer in the prepared baking dish. Layer half the apple mixture on top, followed by half the raisins. Place another third of the bread cubes in another layer on top, followed by the remaining apples and raisins, along with any extra sugar-spice mixture. Layer the remaining bread cubes on top and pour the egg mixture over all, pressing down gently so that the bread absorbs the liquid. Cover with aluminum foil and refrigerate for at least 1 hour or up to overnight.

Pour the water into the Instant Pot® and place the baking dish on the steam rack. Using the handles, lower the dish into the pot. Lock the lid in place and turn the valve to Sealing. Press the Pressure Cook button and set the cook time for 30 minutes at high pressure.

Let the steam release naturally for 15 minutes, then turn the valve to Venting to quick-release any residual steam. Carefully remove the lid and, using the steam rack handles, lift out the pan. Transfer to a cooling rack, remove the foil, and let cool slightly. Cut into wedges and serve.

BONUS STEP *After removing it from the pot, sprinkle the bread pudding with 1 tablespoon of turbinado sugar and bake in a preheated 400°F (200°C) oven until golden brown, about 10 minutes.*

Butter, for greasing

½ cup (100 g) sugar

1 teaspoon cinnamon

2 teaspoons ground cardamom

2 apples (such as Honeycrisp, Gala, Pink Lady, or other crisp varieties), peeled and thinly sliced

2 large eggs

1½ cups (350 ml) whole milk

1 teaspoon pure vanilla extract

Kosher salt

8 oz (225 g) day-old baguette or country bread, cut into 1-inch (2.5-cm) cubes

¼ cup (45 g) raisins

2 cups (475 ml) water

Bosc or Asian pear slices would work well in place of the apples, since they are crisp varieties and can stand up to the pressure.

Experiment with other crunchy toppings, such as toasted sliced almonds, dark chocolate shavings, and candied pecans.

Coconut-Cinnamon Rice Pudding with Toasted Pistachios

Here, a classic, comforting dessert gets an update with fresh flavors and a hands-off cooking method. It's an ideal dish to make ahead and store in the fridge in pretty jars or bowls to have ready for when guests arrive—or for when the urge for a late-night snack comes on.

SERVES 6-8

Select Sauté on the Instant Pot® and add the rice, sugar, 3 teaspoons cinnamon, 1 teaspoon salt, and milk. Bring to a boil, stirring constantly to dissolve the sugar. Press Cancel to reset the program.

Lock the lid in place and turn the valve to Sealing. Press the Pressure Cook button and set the cook time for 18 minutes at low pressure.

Meanwhile, in a small bowl, whisk together the eggs, half-and-half, and vanilla and coconut extracts. Set aside.

Let the steam release naturally for 10 minutes, then turn the valve to Venting to quick-release any residual steam. Press Cancel to reset the program. Carefully remove the lid, add the egg mixture, and stir to combine. Select the Sauté button and cook, stirring occasionally, until the mixture just begins to boil. Press Cancel to reset the program. Stir in the ½ cup (45 g) shredded coconut.

Serve the pudding warm in individual bowls, sprinkled with cinnamon, additional shredded coconut, and pistachios. Or, divide the pudding among individual bowls or jars and let cool completely, then cover and refrigerate for up to 3 days. Just before serving, sprinkle with the toppings.

1½ cups (300 g) Arborio rice

1 cup (200 g) sugar

3 teaspoons ground cinnamon, plus more for garnish

Kosher salt

5 cups (1.2 L) whole milk

2 large eggs

¾ cup (180 ml) half-and-half

1½ teaspoons pure vanilla extract

2 teaspoons coconut extract

½ cup (45 g) unsweetened shredded coconut, plus more for garnish

1 cup (115 g) toasted pistachios, chopped

Chocolate Fudge Cake

A little goes a long way with this super simple chocolate cake, which comes together quickly without any fancy baking tools. A scoop of vanilla ice cream is the perfect partner for the deep, luxurious mocha flavor.

SERVES 6–8

Grease a 7-inch (18-cm) springform pan with butter.

In a small bowl, whisk together the flour, cocoa powder, baking powder, and salt.

In a medium bowl, whisk together the eggs, sugar, melted butter, vanilla, and espresso. Gently whisk the dry mixture into the wet mixture. Fold in the chocolate chips. Pour the mixture into the prepared pan and cover with aluminum foil.

Pour the water into the Instant Pot® and place the springform pan on the steam rack. Using the handles, lower the pan into the pot. Lock the lid in place and turn the valve to Sealing. Press the Pressure Cook button and set the cook time for 35 minutes at high pressure.

Let the steam release naturally for 15 minutes, then turn the valve to Venting to quick-release any residual steam. Carefully remove the lid and, using the steam rack handles, lift out the pan. Transfer to a cooling rack, remove the foil, and let cool completely.

To serve, remove the pan sides, dust the cake with cocoa powder, and cut the cake into wedges. Serve with scoops of vanilla ice cream alongside.

5 tablespoons (70 g) unsalted butter, melted, plus more for greasing

1 cup (115 g) all-purpose flour

¼ cup (20 g) unsweetened cocoa powder, plus more for dusting

1 teaspoon baking powder

¼ teaspoon kosher salt

2 large eggs

1 cup (200 g) granulated sugar

½ teaspoon pure vanilla extract

1 espresso (or 2 tablespoons boiling water mixed with 1 tablespoon instant espresso powder)

8 oz (225 g) semisweet chocolate chips

2 cups (475 ml) water

Vanilla ice cream, for serving

Coffee brings out the flavor of chocolate, so don't skip the espresso in this cake. Freshly brewed and powdered work equally well.

Surprise Lemon Pudding Cake

This popular and intriguing British-inspired dessert is also called self-saucing lemon pudding, because a layer of sweet and tangy lemon curd separates from the fluffy, cloudlike cake on top of it while cooking and acts like a sauce. If you'd like to be very British, pour a little heavy cream over the top of each serving.

SERVES 6–8

Grease with butter a 1½-qt (1.5-L) round ceramic baking dish and a square of aluminum foil large enough to cover it.

Zest and juice the lemons; set aside.

In the bowl of a stand mixer fitted with the paddle attachment, cream the ½ cup (1 stick/115 g) butter, granulated sugar, lemon zest, and a pinch of salt on medium-high speed until pale and fluffy, about 3 minutes. Scrape down the sides of the bowl. One at a time, beat in the egg yolks until fully combined. Add half of the flour and mix on low speed until combined. Add half of the milk, followed by the remaining flour and the remaining milk, mixing until combined after each addition. Add the lemon juice and mix until combined. The batter will be wet.

In a medium bowl, whisk the egg whites until soft peaks form when the whisk is lifted. Gently fold the egg whites into the batter, taking care not to deflate them. Transfer to the prepared baking dish and cover with the prepared aluminum foil.

Pour the water into the Instant Pot® and place the baking dish on the steam rack. Using the handles, lower the dish into the pot. Lock the lid in place and turn the valve to Sealing. Press the Pressure Cook button and set the cook time for 30 minutes at low pressure.

Let the steam release naturally. Carefully remove the lid and, using the steam rack handles, lift out the dish. Transfer to a cooling rack, remove the foil, and let cool slightly. Dust with confectioners' sugar, spoon into individual bowls or plates, and serve with a little heavy cream poured on top, if desired.

½ cup (1 stick/115 g) unsalted butter, at room temperature, plus more for greasing

2 lemons

1 cup (200 g) granulated sugar

Kosher salt

4 large eggs, whites and yolks separated, at room temperature

⅔ cup (75 g) all-purpose flour

2 cups (475 ml) whole milk

2 cups (475 ml) water

Confectioners' sugar, for serving

Heavy cream, for serving (optional)

Mixed Berry Compote

Think of this versatile dessert topping as a fancy jam. It pairs as well with a slice of Meyer Lemon–Gingersnap Cheesecake (page 123) or pound cake as it does spooned over a bowl of vanilla ice cream. Also wonderful at breakfast, it adds a rich flavor to pancakes, waffles, French toast, and plain yogurt.

MAKES ABOUT 2 CUPS (475 ML)

Combine the strawberries, blackberries, sugar, and lemon juice in the Instant Pot®. Lock the lid in place and turn the valve to Sealing. Press the Pressure Cook button and set the cook time for 3 minutes at high pressure.

Let the steam release naturally for 5 minutes, then turn the valve to Venting to quick-release any residual steam. Carefully remove the lid. Press the Cancel button to reset the program.

Press the Sauté button and cook until the berry mixture begins to boil. Stir in the cornstarch mixture and cook, stirring frequently, until the compote has thickened, about 5 minutes. Let cool completely before serving, or transfer to an airtight container and refrigerate for up to 1 week.

2 cups (130 g) strawberries, fresh or frozen (hulled if fresh)

1 cup (140 g) blackberries, fresh or frozen

¾ cup (115 g) sugar

2 tablespoons fresh lemon juice

1 tablespoon cornstarch mixed with 1 tablespoon cold water

Fully Loaded Baked
Potato Soup (page 109)

INDEX

Chocolate Fudge Cake
(page 134)

EVERYDAY INSTANT POT®

Conceived and produced by Weldon Owen, Inc.
in collaboration with Williams Sonoma, Inc.
3250 Van Ness Avenue, San Francisco, CA 94109

A WELDON OWEN PRODUCTION

1045 Sansome Street, Suite 100
San Francisco, CA 94111
www.weldonowen.com

Printed and bound in the USA
First printed in 2018
10 9 8 7 6 5 4 3 2 1

Library of Congress Cataloging-in-Publication
data is available.

ISBN: 978-1-68188-461-5

WELDON OWEN, INC.

President & Publisher Roger Shaw
SVP, Sales & Marketing Amy Kaneko
Finance & Operations Director Thomas Morgan

Associate Publisher Amy Marr
Creative Director Kelly Booth

Art Director & Illustrator Marisa Kwek
Production Designer Howie Severson

Production Director Michelle Duggan
Production Manager Sam Bissell
Imaging Manager Don Hill

Photographer Erin Scott
Food Stylist Lillian Kang
Prop Stylist Glenn Jenkins

Weldon Owen is a division of Bonnier Publishing USA

ACKNOWLEDGMENTS

Weldon Owen wishes to thank the following people for their
generous support in producing this book: Lesley Bruynesteyn,
Sarah Putman Clegg, Josephine Hsu, Rachel Markowitz, Nicola Parisi,
Elizabeth Parson, Emma Rudolph, and Nick Wolf.